Belonging: Rethinking Inclusive Practices to Support Well-Being and Identity

Studies in Inclusive Education

Series Editor
Roger Slee (*University of South Australia, Australia*)

Editorial Board

Mel Ainscow (*University of Manchester, UK*)
Felicity Armstrong (*Institute of Education, University of London, UK*)
Len Barton (*Institute of Education, University of London, UK*)
Suzanne Carrington (*Queensland University of Technology, Australia*)
Joanne Deppeler (*Monash University, Australia*)
Linda Graham (*Queensland University of Technology, Australia*)
Levan Lim (*National Institute of Education, Singapore*)
Missy Morton (*University of Canterbury, New Zealand*)

VOLUME 38

The titles published in this series are listed at *brill.com/stie*

Belonging: Rethinking Inclusive Practices to Support Well-Being and Identity

Edited by

Annie Guerin and Trish McMenamin

BRILL
SENSE

LEIDEN | BOSTON

All chapters in this book have undergone peer review.

The Library of Congress Cataloging-in-Publication Data is available online at http://catalog.loc.gov

Typeface for the Latin, Greek, and Cyrillic scripts: "Brill". See and download: brill.com/brill-typeface.

ISSN 2542-9825
ISBN 978-90-04-38840-6 (paperback)
ISBN 978-90-04-38841-3 (hardback)
ISBN 978-90-04-38842-0 (e-book)

Copyright 2019 by Koninklijke Brill NV, Leiden, The Netherlands.
Koninklijke Brill NV incorporates the imprints Brill, Brill Hes & De Graaf, Brill Nijhoff, Brill Rodopi, Brill Sense, Hotei Publishing, mentis Verlag, Verlag Ferdinand Schöningh and Wilhelm Fink Verlag.
All rights reserved. No part of this publication may be reproduced, translated, stored in a retrieval system, or transmitted in any form or by any means, electronic, mechanical, photocopying, recording or otherwise, without prior written permission from the publisher.
Authorization to photocopy items for internal or personal use is granted by Koninklijke Brill NV provided that the appropriate fees are paid directly to The Copyright Clearance Center, 222 Rosewood Drive, Suite 910, Danvers, MA 01923, USA. Fees are subject to change.

This book is printed on acid-free paper and produced in a sustainable manner.

Printed by Printforce, the Netherlands

Contents

Notes on Contributors VII

1 Introduction: Setting the Scene 1
   Trish McMenamin and Annie Guerin

2 What Happens Next? Inclusion in an Excluding World 5
   Keith Ballard

PART 1
Participation – Belonging in Action

3 Inclusion and Autism
   Belonging 25
   Marie Turner

4 Theory Circles, Inclusion and the PhD student 40
   Be Pannell, Julie White and Fiona Henderson

5 Achieving Citizenship for All: Theorising Active Participation for Disabled Children and Their Families in Early Childhood Education 56
   Kate McAnelly and Michael Gaffney

PART 2
Policy and Theory to Support Belonging

6 The Construction of Giftedness in Education Policy in New Zealand and Australia: Implications for Inclusive Education Policy and Practice 75
   Melanie Wong and Ben Whitburn

7 Employing Intersectionality and the Concept of Difference to Investigate Belonging and Inclusion 95
   Leechin Heng and Julie White

PART 3
Identity and Well-being – Keys to Belonging

8 The Impact of Inclusive Education and Access to Sexuality Education on the Development of Identity in Young People Living with Disability   107
   Henrietta Bollinger and Hera Cook

9 Quality of "Belonging" and its Relationship to Learning: Case Studies of Three New Entrant Children and a 12-Year Old with Down Syndrome   122
   Christine Rietveld

   Index   135

Notes on Contributors

Keith Ballard
is an Emeritus Professor of Education at the University of Otago. He has a background as a teacher, psychologist and researcher. His many publications include work on research methodology; collaboration with parents on disability issues and inclusive education; and analysis of ideas that shape education and social policy.

Henrietta Bollinger
is a writer and Disability advocate. She has a Bachelor of Arts in Sociology and German from Victoria University of Wellington She was a research participant and co-author of an AUT study on the sexuality of young disabled women, published in Disability and Society. She currently works for Disabled Persons Assembly NZ.

Hera Cook
is a historian of sexuality and emotion. Her book *The Long Sexual Revolution: English Women, Sex and Contraception, 1800–1975* (Oxford University Press, 2004), won the 2004 Bonnie and Vern L. Bullough Award from the Foundation for the Scientific Study of Sexuality.

Michael Gaffney
is a lecturer in early childhood education at the College of Education, University of Otago campus, in Dunedin. His interests are in disability studies, childhood and youth studies and the sociology of education.

Annie Guerin
has worked in a variety of teaching roles for over thirty years in primary and secondary schools in New Zealand. Most of this work has been undertaken in rural schools on the west coast of New Zealand's South Island. Most recently Annie has worked as a lecturer at the University of Canterbury. Her work has focussed strongly on inclusive education, assessment, authentic home/school partnerships and establishing cultures of belonging. Annie's work continues to privilege the knowledge of disabled people and their whanau/families as informing a better way forward for education in Aotearoa New Zealand.

Fiona Henderson

is Associate Professor and has worked for 25 years in the university sector, principally in the field of Academic Language and Learning. She has received several national grants for research and teaching related to Academic Literacies and Academic Integrity which have built international relationships and grounded her teaching in China and Vietnam. She received a Carrick Citation in 2007, a Victoria University College Award in 2011 and Victoria University Vice-Chancellor's Awards for Excellence in Programs that Enhance Learning in 2015 and 2016. Her research focuses on internationalisation of the curriculum with Vietnamese, Thai and Chinese partners.

Leechin Heng

is a doctoral candidate at the University of Canterbury. The focus of her research is to explore the meaning-making of inclusion in an initial teacher education programme in Aotearoa New Zealand. Intersectionality of inclusion is one of the main areas she is focusing on in her study. She is also a research assistant for Ennoble, a consultation agency that is involved in research and evaluation for inclusive education in Aotearoa New Zealand.

Kate McAnelly

is a wearer of many hats in the context of inclusive education, as the parent of a disabled child, an early childhood teacher and as a researcher. Her PhD, which she is currently undertaking at the University of Otago College of Education in Dunedin, New Zealand, is examining how the sensory environment in early childhood settings produces the active participation and learning of autistic children. Her research interests of late have also focused on the role and voice of families in inclusive early childhood education.

Trish McMenamin

is a Senior Lecturer at the University of Canterbury. Her research interests include philosophy of education, inclusive education and education policy. She has published articles in these areas in scholarly journals including the Cambridge Journal of Education and Policy Futures in Education.

Be Pannell

examines the nexus between post structural theories and models of adult development in higher education, PhD supervision and coaching psychology. She has a particular interest in the influence of Deleuze and Guattari's philosophy on novel research methodologies and design, that facilitate researchers to perceive connections that may otherwise have gone unnoticed.

She is a research fellow at Victoria University and teaches in the Integrated PhD program and Education.

Christine Rietveld
worked as a kindergarten teacher, after which she took up the position of 'itinerant support teacher' facilitating the inclusion of children with Down Syndrome (DS) into their local early childhood settings as part of the interdisciplinary IHC Early Intervention Programme (now called The Champion Centre at Burwood Hospital, Chch). A PhD concerning the Transition from Preschool to Primary school for Children with DS followed and her work following that has consisted mostly of teaching about inclusive education to tertiary students who are preparing to be teachers. She has published extensively in inclusive early childhood education with a focus on the child's experience and what the theory might look like in practice.

Marie Turner
is currently working on her PhD on Autism and inclusive teaching practices at Victoria University. She has been exposed to autism most of her life. Her brother was diagnosed at the age of five years old. Marie's personal experiences have clearly shaped her interest in working with children diagnosed with Autism Spectrum Disorders and this has led to a rewarding career teaching children on the autism spectrum, many having very complex learning needs.

Ben Whitburn
is an early career researcher and lecturer in inclusive education in the Faculty of Arts and Education at Deakin University. Ben's program of research works the intersection of disability studies in education, policy analysis, and the theory of inclusive education. Ben is an enthusiastic traveller, teacher, and writer. He tweets @BenWhitburn.

Julie White
works as Principal Research Fellow at Victoria University inquiring into inclusive education. She currently leads a large study examining how education works for young people in youth justice systems. She also recently completed a study examining how The Arts can support young people from refugee backgrounds to combat Islamophobia and racism. She has undertaken several investigations about the education of young people who live with chronic health conditions and has written more than 50 scholarly publications about educational inclusion, research methodology and the modernised university.

Melanie Wong is research coordinator in the Faculty of Education and Social Sciences, Manukau Institute of Technology. She is also a PhD candidate at University of Canterbury. Her research interests include gifted education, inclusive education and sociology in education. Mel serves on editorial boards and reviews for journals.

CHAPTER 1

Introduction: Setting the Scene

Trish McMenamin and Annie Guerin

On a winter's weekend in 2016 in Christchurch, New Zealand a range of interested people from near and far gathered to attend The Inclusive Education Summit16. The summit continued a tradition of Australian/New Zealand hui (meetings) that support conversations and initiatives focussed on inclusive practices that recognise and value the humanity of all people. The realisation of human rights and democracy are central to this work. The summit provided an opportunity to explore and rethink notions of inclusion and belonging. Although many of the presentations focussed on inclusive education within schools a broader understanding of belonging provided food for thought across contexts in societal and global communities. The weekend's presentations drew on a mixture of contexts, experiences and cultural concepts as the idea of belonging was investigated. Key questions considered were: What does it mean to belong? Who belongs? Who decides? What do we belong to and what are the implications for those who we think don't belong? Do we want to belong? How do we know if we don't belong? What happens next? These questions provided the foundation for investigations by the authors within this volume.

Belonging is integral to the realisation of inclusion. To belong is to be valued (Smerdon, 2002), to connect with others and to have a sense of fitting in (Osterman, 2000). Educators value developing a culture of belonging to foster a safe environment for risk taking and engagement in learning (MacArthur, 2009; Vygotsky, 1981). Failure to belong has a range of negative implications for identity, health and well-being, academic success and self esteem (Morton, Rietveld, Guerin, McIlroy, & Duke, 2012). Investigating belonging challenges us to investigate notions of fairness, equity and power. Our roles in supporting taken for granted practices are scrutinised as we train a critical eye on the purposes and consequences of such actions. The voices of marginalised people can inform this work as education policies and practices are scrutinised through their lived realities. Personal narratives may provide opportunities to disrupt dominant discourses that privilege certain groups of people while others are marginalised.

Belonging can be understood as a dynamic construct that is shaped by our interactions with people, places and things. There are a range of complexities in both macro and micro settings that support historical constructions that determine access to opportunities for belonging and learning. The impact of pedagogies on shaping these opportunities is a further area for investigation. How do educators support connections between students and their learning? How do they foster opportunities for developing respectful and reciprocal relationships? Are there systemic barriers to these inclusive ways of working and being? How responsive are our uses of curriculum, pedagogy and assessment for the diverse populations of students entering our early childhood education centres, schools and tertiary institutions?

Globally we are experiencing the consequences of decades of neo-liberal ideology as we grapple with policies and practices that continue to marginalise specific groups of people (Ballard, 2012). The knowledges and strengths of some groups of people continue to be privileged in education policies and practices that adhere to narrow constraints and understandings of achievement and success. Some groups of students are supported to know they belong much more easily than others. Paying attention to theoretical perspectives can help us to make sense of how and why this happens – and who benefits from continuing these ways of working. The importance of culturally responsive environments and pedagogies as a more equitable way of working has been well documented in the quest for more inclusive practice (Macfarlane, 2013; Bishop, O'Sullivan, & Berryman, 2010). This volume of work continues the conversation as the participants in TIES 16 present a variety of perspectives that recognise the strength of diversity in everyday practice.

The book is comprised of three parts that respectively examine matters related to participation, policy and theory, and identity and well-being. Each of these three parts serves to draw our attention in different ways to issues, policies and practices that work with and against our attempts to create societies which recognise and acknowledge the many different ways of belonging, and foster respectful and reciprocal relations among people. In their individual chapters the authors examine issues related to inclusive education and belonging across a range of education contexts from early childhood to tertiary education and canvass a variety of topics including issues related to pedagogy, sexuality, theory, policy and practice.

In Chapter 2, Keith Ballard looks into the future and what the next 10 years might hold. He prompts us to consider the exclusion of humanity itself as we grapple or fail to grapple with climate change and the damage we are causing to the world's ecosystems. Ballard argues that we need new thinking about inclusion and belonging which rejects the dominant neoliberal precepts and promotes the language of community and caring, fairness and the public good. The task we face he argues is to reconnect with both the planet and one another; it is, he says, an "urgent task".

Turner, in Chapter 3, turns the focus to ideas about belonging, schooling and the experiences of those with autism spectrum disorders, their families and teachers. In this chapter Turner discusses these matters from her personal perspective as a sibling of a person with autism spectrum disorder and from her professional perspective as a teacher. In the chapter, the author uses the ethnographic approach of story-telling (Clandinin & Caine, 2013) to explore the concepts of inclusion and belonging in what is a thoughtful and different perspective on what belonging might mean. In Chapter 4, Pannell, White and Henderson move away from the compulsory schooling years to consider inclusion at the tertiary level. The authors present a discussion about what inclusion and belonging might mean in the context of the relationship between PhD students and the academy. The authors challenge dominant ideas about and constructions of the PhD student as the isolated, independent subject. In Chapter 5 McAnelly and Gaffney also focus on the non-compulsory sector but at the other end of the spectrum, that of the early childhood years. This chapter also draws on the personal experience of one of the authors which serves as the impetus for thinking about and challenging oppression and oppressive practices that deny children and their families their right to belong and actively participate in educational communities. The authors, echoing Ballard's view to the future, want more for families than that they can only imagine better futures for their children. Familes, they argue, they must be able to realise this too as this is simply what they deserve. Wong and Whitburn turn their thoughts in Chapter 6 to how policy positions in Australia and New Zealand construct giftedness and/or twice-exceptionality in ways that can marginalise and have a negative effect on the experiences of children and their families. The authors share the voices of parents who speak about their experiences with schooling. Wong and Whitburn argue that the inclusiveness of education for these children is limited by reductive and limited assumptions and understandings of giftedness. In Chapter 7 the discussion turns to matters of theory. Heng and White set out a theoretical framework for thinking about belonging and inclusion. Like Ballard, Heng and White argue that we need to think differently and form the discourse around inclusion and belonging differently. In the chapter they ask us to consider how the concept of intersectionality might help us to think differently and to move away from what they describe as the assumptions of the need to in someway join the maintream or the norm that are inherent in the terms "belonging" and "inclusion". In Chapter 8 Bollinger and Cook also challenge us to consider issues of identity by drawing our attention to the idea of what they call the intertwined identity for some who see themselves as both able and disabled. Bollinger and Cook report on the views of a group of young adults with congential disablities as regards their experiences of secondary inclusive education, Sexuality Education and how these shaped their sexuality as young adults post-school. The chapter offers compelling insights into an area that has had little attention and raises new issues as regards what belonging means in the context of sexuality, disability and identity. In the final chapter of the book Rietveld reports on the experiences of belonging in the primary school for some children with Down Syndrome. Rietveld argues that it is critical for their learning that children belong as valued and integral members of their educational setting. Through her description of the experiences of the children, Rietveld explores and demonstrates the subtleties of what it means to belong, the ways in which belonging is subverted and how the quality of belonging is shaped by the school culture and norms.

Together these chapters make up a unique collection of material examining matters to do with inclusion and belonging. They raise issues that are provocative and challenging, and offer new insights into how we might conceptualise belonging and inclusion in our ever-changing world.

CHAPTER 2

What Happens Next? Inclusion in an Excluding World

Keith Ballard

The invitation to write this chapter asked me to consider some of the issues we might face in the next ten years. Looking into the future is at best a speculative task, so I have chosen to look at areas that have so far proven to be especially resistant to inclusionary efforts. These warrant our ongoing attention because they are embedded in systems of power that have yet to be effectively challenged.

I also want to question what inclusion is and may become as we involve ourselves in the idea of inclusion as a social justice project. As Tony Booth (Personal Communication, 27 June, 2000) has asked, what is it that we are to be included in? What kind of communities, society and planet earth are we working toward? At present we live with the possible exclusion of humanity itself as we damage our ecosystems and fail to act on climate change. I will examine how the ideas of neoliberal individualism contribute to this situation and suggest how we might develop more inclusive policies and practices by an emphasis on collaboration and interdependence.

1 The Idea of Inclusion

Inclusion implies that someone has been excluded and that some are able to prevent others from participation in significant cultural, economic, and political activities. The work of inclusion may then be seen as a process of identifying and removing barriers to participation in society and its institutions (Booth & Ainscow, 2012). Such barriers typically involve discrimination on the basis of disability, ethnicity, gender, sexuality and poverty. Those with power use their control of resources, ideas and language to limit the experiences of others.

To examine issues of inclusion and exclusion requires that we identify what ideas are chosen to shape our world; what beliefs and values are referred to as justifying the rightness of those ideas; and who has the power to have their ideas enacted in everyday life. As the New Zealand Disability Strategy (Minister for Disability Issues, 2001) says, disability happens "when one group of people create barriers by designing a world only for their way of living" (p. 3). In a similar way poverty, inequality and damaging exploitation of the environment happens when one group has the power to enact their preferences in ways that enhance their own wellbeing.

Looking forward 10 years it would be good to think that we might have a clearer definition of inclusion, one that encompasses explicit justification of the philosophical, ethical, theoretical and values positions that form the basis for inclusion work. Nevertheless, I think that the challenge to clarify a definition should not inhibit inclusion work but rather should require that reading and thinking about what inclusion is should be a core part of how we do that work. Paulo Freire (1998) said that in order to work against oppression we must apply "intellectual rigour" (p. 4) to our analysis of exclusionary practices and to the justification for our involvement in change. For each of the issues I identify in this paper I suggest the need to examine the sociopolitical context, theoretical assumptions and ideology behind both the issues and the more inclusive alternatives that we may propose. A simple turn to the claims of evidence based practice is not sufficient because as Linda Tuhiwai Smith (2013) says in writing about poverty in New Zealand, "[e]vidence is only powerful if the powerful accept its 'truth'" (p. 228) and truth is framed by our experiences and beliefs.

2   Inclusion and Democracy

In a democracy citizens decide by vote who should govern and what laws and regulations should be used to organise society. Power is said to be in the hands of the people and this would seem to imply the inclusion of all in participatory decision making (Brown, 2015).

Nevertheless, in New Zealand, as elsewhere, women have had to struggle to ensure their place as enfranchised citizens and continue to be underrepresented in parliament and other areas. Māori also have experience of being denied the vote. They have had their land taken from them and continue to seek their rights under the Treaty of Waitangi, the agreement Māori made with the English Crown in 1840 that allowed for colonial settlement. In such examples it is evident that democratic power is not necessarily shared on an equitable basis.

Disabled people are another group that strive to have their wishes and rights acknowledged. For example, disability advocates have said that the Ministry of Health is acting illegally by refusing to pay family who take on the role of carers for disabled adult family members. The courts have agreed with them saying that the ban on these payments "discriminates against people on the basis of their family status" (Human Rights Commission, 2016, p. 1). The government's response was to pass under urgency an Amendment to the Health and Disability Act that prohibits payments to family members and will not allow any claim that this is discriminatory (Human Rights Commission, 2016).

Constitutional lawyer Geoffrey Palmer (2016) says that the ability of the New Zealand government to pass a law in this way, sometimes with a majority of one vote, is an example of what he calls 'unbridled power'. He notes that New Zealand is unlike other democracies in two main respects. First, we do not have an upper house or equivalent mechanism to monitor and place limits on executive (Cabinet) power. Second, NZ is one of only three democracies (with the UK and Israel) that do not have a written constitution. The Cabinet manual (Cabinet Office, 2008) explains that our constitution "is to be found in formal legal decisions, in decisions of the courts and in practices" (p. 1). Palmer (2016) describes this as a fragmented arrangement not accessible to most people and readily changed by government action. He proposes that we should have a written constitution that sets out our core rights and values and includes a Bill of Rights and the Treaty of Waitangi. Legislation thought to be inconsistent with the constitution could be examined in the courts and if deemed to be unconstitutional struck down by the courts.

To encourage public discussion on these issues Geoffrey Palmer and Andrew Butler (2016) have published a version of what they think a written constitution could look like. As a contribution to this discussion we might suggest how the ideas and values of inclusion could be embedded in a constitutional document that could be used for teaching and advocacy and that would have the power of democratic adoption and legal standing. A written constitution could support the profound changes in policy and practice that are needed if a more inclusive society is to become a constitutional and lived reality.

3 Violence by Men against Women

The Family Violence Death Review Committee (FVDRC) advises the Health Quality and Safety Commission on how to reduce the number of family violence deaths. The FVDRC (2016) notes that New Zealand women experience a higher rate of domestic violence than women in 14 other Organisation of Economic Cooperation and Development (OECD) countries. The data show that this violence is also linked to child abuse.

In a Universal Periodic Review on human rights the United Nations has noted that New Zealand has "high rates of child poverty [and] violence against women and children" (Amnesty International, 2016, p. 7). The Women's Refuge Statistical Report for 2014–2015 (Women's Refuge, 2016, pp. 23–24) records from police data 33,209 domestic violence incidents reported in that year; police attended 200 domestic violence situations a day; and police estimate that only 18% of domestic violence incidents are reported. Women's Refuge recorded that on average 201 women and children needed a safe place to sleep each night.

A report by the UK government's Department for International Development records that "[v]iolence against women and girls is the most widespread form of abuse worldwide affecting…one third of all women globally in their lifetime (Alexander-Scott, Bell, & Holden, 2016, p. 4). The United Nations (1993, p. i) has said such violence is a "serious human rights violation" (p. i) and that this reflects a wider context of "sexual and economic inequality in society" involving pervasive male power in which "women are kept in a position of inferiority to men" (p. 10). In New Zealand inequality in income between men and women and expectations regarding appearance and behaviour suggest that men exert control over the lives of women and girls. A highly commercialised and sexualised media plays a role in normalising a world that is not equally designed by women and men for a shared way of living.

If inclusion is about breaking down barriers to participation then in this context it is not possible to see New Zealand as an inclusive society for women and girls at this time. Across all areas of society women are active in identifying and challenging restrictions on their freedom and opportunities. Reports such as that of the Ministry of Women's Affairs (2013) identify strategies for preventing domestic violence. The need for men in particular to challenge sexist language and actions at every level of society and across cultural and belief systems is also indicated. Yet on present evidence it seems likely that male power over women and male violence against women may continue to be on the agenda for inclusion and social justice activism in ten years' time.

4 Inclusion and the Treaty of Waitangi

The Treaty of Waitangi was signed in 1840 between Governor William Hobson for the Crown and about 540 Māori chiefs. The Treaty promised Māori the possession of their lands, forests and fisheries and the right to manage their own affairs. As coloniser settlement increased these agreements were soon broken. Māori land was stolen, the Treaty ignored, and Māori became impoverished and alienated.

From the 1970's moves have been made for recognition of the Treaty. The establishment in 1975 of the Waitangi Tribunal provided a mechanism for discussion and resolution of Māori claims under the Treaty. The Cabinet Manual (Cabinet Office, 2008) now states that the constitution "increasingly reflects the fact that the Treaty of Waitangi is regarded as a founding document of government in New Zealand" (p. 1). In an article on the Treaty in New Zealand law Janine Hayward (1997) quotes Justice Richardson in a 1987 Court of Appeal case saying that "the Treaty must be viewed as a solemn compact between two identified parties, the Crown and Māori, through which the colonisation of New Zealand became possible" (p. 477). A New Zealand Catholic Bishops Conference stated that "In the Treaty of Waitangi we find the moral basis for our presence in Aotearoa New Zealand" (The Catholic Church in Aotearoa New Zealand, 2010).

Nevertheless, there is significant public opposition to recognition of the Treaty and constitutional lawyer Mai Chen anticipates that opposition to the Treaty may create major problems in negotiating a written constitution that recognises Treaty obligations (Chen, 2005).

Speaking openly against Māori and the Treaty became more evident following a speech by Don Brash at Orewa in 2004 (Hager, 2006, pp. 79–96). As leader of the National party at the time, Brash (2004) described Māori as "having a culture of dependence and grievance" and said that Māori gained special privileges from government funding based on race. Brash suggested that there were no "full blooded Māori", a reference to the idea of blood purity that is a basis for eugenics. In an editorial, the *Sydney Morning Herald* referred to these statements by Brash as "playing the race card" and said that "[t]he liberation of racist...views from the constraints on which social cohesion relies is not easy to reverse" (Editorial, 2004, p. 12).

The Brash speech and its claims that Māori were a privileged group was popular. Even though Brash and his supporters could not identify examples of the claimed privileges, the speech was associated with a 20% increase in voter support for the National Party (Hager, 2006, p. 79). The Labour led government of the time reacted by aligning with such views. Labour had recently legislated to prevent Māori seeking judgement in the courts regarding a significant Treaty issue and then moved to require that policy areas should not be associated specifically with data on Māori deprivation (Hager, 2006, p. 94).

In health and in epidemiological research life expectancy is regarded as a key indicator of how well a society cares for its people and therefore as a strong indicator of inclusion (Wilkinson, 2005). The Ministry of Health and University of Otago (2006) have used census and health data to report on what they term the 1981 to 1999 'decades of disparity'. These were the years when neoliberal ideology was embedded into economic and social policies in New Zealand creating an increasingly unequal society. The data show that in this period Māori, who already had higher mortality rates, experienced a decline in life expectancy in comparison with non-Māori. Disparity in life expectancy at birth increased from six to seven years in the early 1980's to eight to nine years by 1999 (Ministry of Health & University of Otago, 2006, p. xi).

The Ministry and University researchers reported that the increase in socio-economic inequality for Māori in comparison with non-Māori in this period explains up to half the observed disparity in life expectancy between the two groups. Life style variables – including smoking, diet and alcohol consumption – were found to contribute less than 10% of the variance, negating a deficit interpretation of the data (p. 59). Also, inequality in life expectancy was evident within socio-economic groups indicating that socio-economic position alone was not the major health impact. Rather, the researchers say that "discrimination and socio-economic position are closely intertwined" reflecting a "racialised social order" in which health inequalities are the result of inequalities of resources and power (Ministry of Health & University of Otago, 2006, p. 4). Given the history of these issues and the ongoing disparity of Māori – Non Māori life expectancy at birth (Ministry of Social Development, 2016) it seems likely they will require ongoing attention.

5   Inclusion and the Neoliberal State

The adoption of neoliberal ideas and values across many countries is the result of the successful promotion of individualism and market fundamentalism as the proper basis for human relationships. The neoliberal model of humans is that we are all "self-interested utility maximisers" (Olssen, 2002, p. 14). That is, we are expected to act for our own benefit, and deemed unlikely to support others in collective action or to endorse inclusive values such as empathy and interdependence.

If we are to pursue a more inclusive society we need to understand where neoliberal ideas come from and how they have become central to government policy in New Zealand and elsewhere. The answers are to be found in an historical struggle of ideas about how society should be organised and in whose interests. At times the idea of the individual good, the market and a minimal role for the state become dominant. At other times the the emphasis is on the idea of the social good and a state with responsibility for the well being of all.

Prior to 1984 New Zealand had followed a trend beginning in the 1930's that saw many nations moving away from the free market economics of Adam Smith

(1723–1790) and toward the ideas of John Maynard Keynes (1883–1946). Historian David Harvey (2007) records American president Franklin Roosevelt telling Congress in 1935 that "excessive market freedoms lay at the root of the economic and social problems of the 1930's depression" and that wealth gained from "excessive profits creates undue private power" (p. 183).

In response to the crisis of those times Roosevelt turned to the ideas of Keynes who believed that the state had a responsibility to act for the wider social good in ways that private market wealth would not do. Keynesian economics involve a form of "managed capitalism" (Lansley, 2012, p. 34). This includes the regulation of markets to inhibit excessive financial speculation and monopoly power; progressive taxation that provides welfare to mitigate hunger and poverty; promoting full employment; and supporting unions and other forms of collective action (Lansley, 2012). A fairer inclusion of everyone in society is the goal although, as George Packer (2013) has noted, in many of these contexts women and minorities have still struggled against their oppression.

Regulatory controls on markets and progressive taxation for the social good reduced the money and power available to those with wealth who supported the economic ideas of Adam Smith. Smith argued that individuals should have maximum freedom for their activities and should not be impeded by the state. He claimed that when people were driven by the profit motive market forces would ensure "efficient outcomes *as if by an invisible hand*" (Stiglitz, 2003, p. 73, italics in original). Economist Joseph Stiglitz (2003) says that neoliberalism is based on this "simplistic model of the market" in which Adam Smith's invisible hand is believed to work so that an unregulated market will be self-correcting (p. 74).

A key figure in promoting neoliberalism was Austrian economist Friedrich von Hayek (1899–1992) who opposed Keynesian ideas and argued instead for Adam Smith's self-seeking individual to be allowed to operate free of restrictions. In 1947, at the village of Mont Pelerin in Switzerland, Hayek established the Mont Pelerin Society as a focus for encouraging governments to adopt free market policies. David Harvey (2007) records Hayek saying that the Mont Pelerin Society needed to engage in "the battle for ideas" and that it could take "at least a generation for that battle to be won" (p. 21).

The Mont Pelerin Society continues today as a centre for advocating a minimal state; low taxation, to ensure that the state has limited resources for state activities; welfare is to be opposed; the focus of the state is to be on the protection of private property; all other activities, including education and health, should be privatised; the bargaining power of labour and the unions is to be reduced; and individual and market activities should be deregulated (Harvey, 2007). Globalisation is the process that advocates for these ideas internationally making neoliberalism seem a normative consensus across nations.

Hayek's notion of a "battle for ideas" was also recognised by an American, Lewis Powell, who identified education as a key strategy for promoting the free market. Powell recommended the establishment of private research agencies and think tanks that would ensure a strong media and public presence for neoliberalism (Giroux, 2009). Henry Giroux (2009) writes that Powell set out his ideas in a Memo that had a significant impact and saw individuals and groups donate around "$3 billion over a thirty year period" (p. 4) to establish a network of institutions, such as the Heritage Foundation and The American Enterprise Institute, along with university chairs, especially in economics and law, at major universities, all of which were to become a powerful voice for the right.

In this regard the University of Chicago School of Economics, headed by Milton Freidman, has been a major influence in advocating for neoliberal economic and social policies (Lansley, 2012). Friedman, who has served as president of the Mont Pelerin Society, urges governments to abandon Keynesian ideas and to set in place an emphasis on individualism, private property and market processes.

Economist Brian Easton (1997) has referred to the New Zealand Treasury as following an "extreme version" of Chicago School neoliberalism (p. 93). The Mont Pelerin Society has a substantive presence in New Zealand, supported by individuals – for example, economist and politician Don Brash has hosted several visits to New Zealand by Milton Freidman (Hager, 2006, p. 72) – and groups such as The New Zealand Centre for Political Research, The Centre for Independent Studies, and The New Zealand Initiative. Their ideas have been evident in the polices of both major political parties, Labour and National, reducing attention to the social good and creating a society in which collaboration and inclusion is less in evidence while deregulation and the privatisation of state functions has moved power and control away from the influence of the electorate and into individual and corporate hands (Rashbrook, 2015). The present National government has, for example, stated its belief in "small government" (English, 2015) and has accepted Treasury advice that "[w]here possible the government will favour private markets for the provision and ownership of infrastructure" including hospitals and schools (Treasury, 2015, p. 50). In the neoliberal state all human needs are to be available for commercial profit (Brown, 2015).

From the time that a Labour government introduced neoliberalism in 1984 its continued application has seen New Zealand record one of the highest levels of income inequality in the developed world (Wilkinson & Pickett, 2009). High levels of income inequality are associated with inequality in health and life expectancy, less empathy and concern for the public good, and increases in antisocial behaviours (Chang, 2014; Lansley, 2012; Wilkinson & Picket, 2009).

High levels of child poverty and low levels of child-care in comparison with other developed countries have been noted regularly in United Nations reports on New Zealand (UNICEF, 2016) while Russell Wills, a paediatrician and Children's Commissioner, has said that "Third World diseases...have become an everyday occurrence" amongst our child population (Chapman, 2013). Health researcher Robin Gauld has noted that these "diseases of poverty", including rheumatic heart disease, have been "virtually eradicated" from most developed countries (Gibb, 2013, p. 1).

In response to such concerns the Children's Commissioner convened an Expert Advisory Group to suggest ways to help the 25% of the nations children identified as living in poverty. The Expert Advisory Group (Boston & McIntosh, 2012) said that these children were "excluded from the normal patterns of modern life" through "material deprivation and hardship" (p. 1) and in its recommendations to the government identified as one essential strategy the introduction of a universal benefit for children under six years of age. The report provided an economic analysis on how this could be afforded and why, in economic terms, it would work. They emphasised that in addition to providing financial support for children a universal benefit would send the important signal that all children are to be valued and supported by the state, that is, by all of us, an inclusive commitment. The universal benefit was rejected by the government with Prime Minister John Key calling it a "dopey idea" (Boston & Chapple, 2014, p. 103) although such a benefit is available to every New Zealand citizen over 65 years of age (St. John, 2014).

In a 'state of the children' report the United Nations Children's Fund (UNICEF, 2016) includes deaths per thousand children from birth to five years of age, an indicator of how well a society cares for its children. New Zealand has 6 deaths per 1000 children which is more than the rate for 37 other high income countries (for example, UK 4, Australia 4, Norway 3, Finland 2, p. 111). The report says that high child mortality rates are related to "cycles of deprivation that are transmitted from one generation to the next, deepening inequality that threatens societies everywhere" and notes that this can be remediated by changes to policy and public spending (UNICEF, 2016, p. 2).

In the neoliberal view public spending on welfare is not a social good supporting those in need but indicates a failure of the individual for being unable to sustain themselves. The term 'welfare dependency' is used to name those on welfare. This ignores social conditions such as a shortage of jobs and low wages and implies that those in need show a personal moral failing by being dependent on help much as one can be dependent on alcohol or drugs. This was the basis for the severe cuts in welfare payments of 10 to 30 per cent made by a National government in 1991 (Boston & Chapple, 2014, p. 64) and identified in research as the cause of a significant and ongoing increase in children living in poverty (Blaiklock et al., 2002, p. 8). A belief in welfare dependency is also the reason that a subsequent Labour government, while raising benefits for some categories of those in need, did not restore benefits to previous levels. Child poverty continues as a feature of life in New Zealand.

Wendy Brown (2015) writes that neoliberalism "applies economic values and practices to every dimension of human life" transforming people "from thoughtful citizens to human capital" (p. 24). The International Monetary Fund (IMF) has promoted neoliberalism across the globe yet its research has shown that nations following this agenda have experienced limited economic growth together with economic instability and levels of inequality that harm social wellbeing (Ostry, Loungani, & Furceri, 2016). In this context work toward more inclusive societies would seem justified.

Environmentalist George Monbiot (2016) suggests that whatever happens next it should not involve a simplistic turn to the Keynesian economics of the 1930's to 1970's era. While in that time private wealth was constrained and general social wellbeing pursued Monbiot argues that these economies relied on promoting consumer demand to drive economic growth. To pursue this approach would involve ongoing environmental destruction and global warming. Monbiot says that what we urgently need now is deeper thought about both social and environmental justice. In this regard Bronwyn Hayward (2012) proposes a "new political imagination for citizenship" involving "human connectedness and interdependence" (p. 151) together with ecological responsibility to create "a more just, democratic and sustainable future" (p. 152). This would seem an inclusive goal to work for over the next ten years.

6   Education as a Commodity

In 1987 a Labour government accepted Treasury advice that education is not a social good but a private good. Education should therefore be seen as a commodity to be "traded in the market place" (Grace, 1988, p. 5). The state education system was radically changed so that each school became an education 'provider' competing for students and shaped by a language of commerce in which schools are audited, there is a stock-take of the curriculum, and parents are consumers.

This market based school system has seen an increase in disparities between richer and poorer schools and an increase in ethnic segregation across schools (Wylie, 2012). These are the effects of a system that can never be inclusive because it is designed to set children, parents and teachers apart as competing individuals pursuing a private good in the market place. This fragmented system is described by Cathy Wylie (2012) as "lacking a shared purpose" (p. 106). It is a system that has made it difficult for parents of disabled children to establish inclusion policies that would be enacted across all schools. Cathy Wylie (2102) suggests that we need to restore an infrastructure of "vital connections" for state schools that would support teachers in the "collective creation of new knowledge through joint work [and]...shared understandings" (Wylie, 2012, p. 75).

To create inclusive education a new system is needed. This would be grounded in the democratic idea of education for the social good and the inclusive idea of classroom practice undertaken as the practice of social justice (Freire, 1998). As part of such a move we need to bring children back into the language of our work. If we talk of learners we construct our role as a process focused on predetermined outcomes. The terminology of learners reflects what Wendy Brown (2015) describes as the "deep antihumanism" of "neoliberal rationality" (p. 222). If we talk of children we refer to a wider and more complex teacher role in the development of young lives.

The market model was introduced to tertiary education in the early 1990's. Competition had a particular effect on teacher training seeing an increase from six institutions to 32 mostly private agencies offering over 100 programmes (Alcorn, 1999). Unlike professions such as medicine and law New Zealand teachers do not have to qualify in a university setting. Also, pressure on institutions to compete for students has seen the duration of pre-service primary training lowered from around four years to one year. The long term consequences of this move can only be to erode teacher knowledge and their ability to understand the theory and practice of their field.

In a study across four years of 93 young New Zealand people Karen Nairn, Jane Higgins, and Judith Sligo (2012) found that a neoliberal environment offered "persuasive messages about what is valued" (p. 177) and that the children of the market had taken "up the language of free choice and self-responsibility" (p. 176). If each of us is on our own in the market places of education and society then for those who believe in inclusion it is not clear what it is that people are to be included in. The self seeking individual may not, for example, care a great deal about those who are poor, disabled or discriminated against. Such a lack of care may be evident in the success politicians have had in gaining voter support by targeting hostile feelings against minority groups and those living in poverty (Hager, 2006, pp. 85–87). Roger Slee (2011) refers to the emergence of a "collective indifference to the excluded" suggesting a lack of social cohesion that threatens the idea of a society in which all belong (p. 48).

7   Climate Change: Excluding Ourselves

Since 1958 the US National Oceanic Atmospheric Administration working in collaboration with the Scripps Institution of Oceanography have measured the level of carbon dioxide in the atmosphere. Measures made in May 2013 showed that "[f]or the first time in human history, the concentration of climate-warming carbon dioxide has passed the milestone level of 400 parts per million" (Carrington, 2013). Bob Watson, a former chair of the International Panel on Climate Change (IPCC), stated that this increase reaches a level of CO_2 not seen for several million years and will result in "an increase in surface temperature of 3C-5C compared to pre-industrial times", creating a climate in which humans cannot survive (Carrington, 2013).

American National Aeronautics and Space Administration (NASA) data show that in January 2016 global temperatures were "between 1.15C and 1.4C" above the preindustrial average while Arctic temperatures were so high through the winter that an expert on Arctic climate, Mark Sorreze, described them as extreme and "absurd" (Mathiesen, 2016). Less than 0.1 per cent of this warming came from an El Nino weather pattern, and overall we are close to the 1.5C of warming that the IPCC says that we should not exceed.

Nevertheless, speaking at a meeting of the Mont Pelerin Society, Vaclav Klaus (2008) declared that an "important part" of the Society's agenda was to oppose the ideas of climate change. Klaus said that "warming alarmism" comes from environmentalism that he described as a "freedom and prosperity...destroying ideology". Think tanks aligned with the Mont Pelerin Society promote a similar view. Gus Speth (2008) records that the American Enterprise Institute, Heritage Foundation and the Cato Institute began opposition to environmentalism in the 1970's (p. 81) and since then have established a substantial "disinformation industry" with the Heritage Foundation stating that the environmental movement is the "greatest single threat to the American economy" (p. 82).

Nicholas Stern, a former chief economist and senior vice president at the World Bank, does not support this view. In his report to the UK government on the economics of climate change Stern wrote that climate change was "the greatest and widest-ranging market failure ever seen", a planet consuming itself (Stern, 2006, p. i). His panel of economists calculated that the financial cost of preventing further global warming was much less than the cost of allowing carbon emissions to continue. Nevertheless, as Naomi Oreskes and Erik Conway (2010) show, neoliberal think tanks such as the Competitive Enterprise Institute in America continue to reject climate science and describe environmentalism as a "socialist front" (Oreskes & Conway, 2010, p. 252). Such ideas help perpetuate what Rob Nixon (2011) calls 'slow violence', the gradual accumulation of deep harm to the planet and humanity that is the result of climate change.

The term Anthropocene is used to describe the present geological epoch of Anthropogenic Climate Change. This is an age in which for the first time in the history of the Earth one organism, the human, is responsible for profound changes to the ecological conditions of the entire planet. These changes are leading to the extinction of a wide range of life forms, each extinction changing further the ecologies that sustain Earth in its present form. From work with scientists studying the high ongoing rate of loss of animal and plant life Elizabeth Kolbert (2014) explains how we are inside the Sixth Great Extinction, driving us to the kind of fundamental changes that previously occurred millions of year ago as a result of catastrophic events such as a meteor strike.

The present circumstances of global warming and environmental degradation are described by Naomi Klein (2014) as the result of an ideology of individualism, consumption and greed. She suggests that our survival will involve developing ideas of "the collective...the communal...the commons...and the civic" (p. 460), moving from selfishness towards shared responsibility for the wellbeing of all. In New Zealand (Oldham, 2016) and internationally (Klein, 2014) there are examples of people working collaboratively and effectively on social justice and on climate issues supporting an inclusive agenda. What happens next will depend on such work.

8 Belonging

Oxfam International (2016) tells us that the world we belong to includes 62 people who have the same wealth as half (3.5 billion) of the world's population. These 62 people have seen their wealth increase by 44 per cent since 2010 while in the same period there has been a drop of 41 per cent in the wealth of half of humanity. Data from New Zealand and other nations that follow neoliberal ideology show a similar pattern of inequality and poverty. Statistics New Zealand (2016) reports that 10 percent of New Zealand individuals have 60 percent of all wealth while the poorest 40 percent hold 3 percent of total wealth. The wealthy gain increasing power while many people experience what John Ralston Saul (2009) describes as a "return to the unsecured cheap labour of...over a century ago" (p. 149) with declining salaries and wages (Rashbrook, 2015, p. 40). In such ways neoliberalism erodes democracy from within (Brown, 2015, p. 18).

Climate science shows that in the world we belong to human actions directly affect every part of our environment, from atmosphere to ocean currents and from weather patterns to the kind of plants and animals that live along with us. We are not separate from these elements of life on earth because, as geographer Noel Castree (2016) says, human activities have become fused with nature. Castree suggests that in this context the social sciences and humanities are as important as the biophysical sciences because our focus needs to be on changing our beliefs, ideologies and institutions so that we can live in more inclusive ways. Art historian and curator Susan Ballard (2015) suggests that we might learn from the work of artists who are developing ideas of nature as an inclusive system "of environmental and interspecies relationships" (p. 71), imagining new possibilities for a time of radical change.

New thinking about inclusion and belonging cannot be done with the language of the neoliberal belief system. An ideology is carried in its language and as the poet and activist Audre Lorde (1984) advised, 'the masters tools will never dismantle the masters house'. Alternative ideas can only exist and be shared through an alternative language that speaks of collaboration and interdependence rather than of competition and individualism. A language of community, the commons, union, caring, fairness, public service, taxation for social wellbeing and of education as a social good can frame a new discourse within which we can challenge exclusion and work with ideas of inclusion. We might see this as an urgent task of reconnection with our planet and with one-another.

References

Alcorn, P. (1999). Initial teacher education since 1990: Funding and supply as determinants of policy and practice. *New Zealand Journal of Educational Studies, 34*(2), 110–120.

Alexander-Scott, M., Bell, E., & Holden, J. (2016). *DFID guidance note: Shifting social norms to tackle Violence Against Women and Girls (VAWG)*. London: VAWG Helpdesk.

Amnesty International. (2016). *Annual report*. Auckland: Amnesty International New Zealand.

Ballard, S. (2015). Signal eight times: Nature, catastrophic extinction events and contemporary art. *Reading Room: A Journal of Art and Culture, 7*, 70–95.

Blaiklock, A., Kiro, C., Belgrave, M., Low, W., Davenport, E., & Hassal, I. (2002). *When the invisible had rocks the cradle: New Zealand children in a time of change* (Innocenti Working Paper No. 93). Florence: Innocenti Research Centre.

Booth, T., & Ainscow, M. (2012). *Index for inclusion: Developing learning and participation in schools* (2nd ed.). Bristol: Centre for Studies in Inclusive Education.

Boston, J., & Chapple, S. (2014). *Child poverty in New Zealand.* Wellington: Bridget Williams Books.

Boston, J., & McIntosh, T. (2012). *Solutions to child poverty in New Zealand: Evidence for action.* Wellington: Children's Commissioner. Retrieved from http://www.occ.org.nz/assets/Uploads/EAG/Final-report/Final-report-Solutions-to-child-poverty-evidence-for-action.pdf

Brash, D. (2004). *Orewa speech: Nationhood.* Retrieved from http://www.scoop.co.nz/stories/PA0401/S00220.htm

Brown, W. (2015). *Undoing the demos: Neoliberalism's stealth revolution.* New York, NY: Zone Books.

Cabinet Office. (2008). *Cabinet manual.* Wellington: Department of the Prime Minister and Cabinet. Retrieved from https://cabinetmanual.cabinetoffice.govt.nz/files/manual.pdf

Carrington, D. (2013). *Carbon dioxide in atmosphere passes milestone level.* Retrieved from http://www.theguardian.com/environment/2013/may/10/carbon-dioxide-highest-level-greenhouse-gas

Castree, N. (2016). Unfree radicals: Geoscientists, the anthropocene and left politics. *Antipode, 49,* 52–74. doi:10.1111/antia.12187

Chang, H.-J. (2014). *Economics: A user's guide.* London: Penguin Books.

Chapman, K. (2013). *Children need changes now – commissioner.* Retrieved from http://i.stuff.co.nz/dominion-post/news/8169594/Children-need-changes-now-commissioner

Chen, M. (2005). *Unbridled power will be redistributed.* Retrieved from http://www.nzherald.co.nz/nz/news/article.cfm?c_id=1&objectid=10118060

Easton, B. (1997). *The commercialisation of New Zealand.* Auckland: Auckland University Press.

Editorial. (2004, March 8). The New Zealand race card. *The Sydney Morning Herald.*

English, W. (2015). *Annual John Howard lecture: Menzies research centre, Melbourne.* Retrieved from https://www.beehive.govt.nz/speech/annual-john-howard-lecture-menzies-research-centre

Family Violence Death Review Committee. (2016). *Fifth annual report: Agencies need to change response to family violence.* Retrieved from http://www.hqsc.govt.nz/publications-and-resources/publication/2434/

Freire, P. (1998). *Teachers as cultural workers: Letters to those who dare to teach.* Boulder, CO: Westview Press.

Gibb, J. (2013, January 16). Public health issues need tackling: Prof. *Otago Daily Times.* Retrieved from http://www.odt.co.nz/news/national/242630/public-health-issues-need-tackling-prof

Giroux, H. (2009, May 20). The Powell memo and the teaching machines of right-wing extremists. *Truthout.* Retrieved from http://archive.truthout.org/100109A

Grace, G. (1988). *Education: Commodity or public good?* Wellington: Victoria University Press.

Hager, N. (2006). *The hollow men: A study in the politics of deception.* Nelson: Craig Potton Publishing.

Harvey, D. (2007). *A brief history of neoliberalism.* Oxford: Oxford University Press.

Hayward, B. (2012). *Children, citizenship and environment: Nurturing a democratic imagination in a changing world.* London: Routledge.

Hayward, J. (1997). *Appendix: The principles of the treaty of Waitangi.* Retrieved from http://www.justice.govt.nz/tribunals/waitangi-tribunal/treaty-of-waitangi/tribunals/waitangi-tribunal/documents/public/treaty-principles-appendix-99

Human Rights Commission. (2016). *Caring for a disabled adult family member.* Retrieved from https://www.hrc.co.nz/enquiries-and-complaints/faqs/caring-disabled-adult-family-members/

Klaus, V. (2008). *Current global warming alarmism and the Mont Pelerin society's long term agenda.* Retrieved from http://Klaus.cz/clanky/1206

Klein, N. (2014). *This changes everything: Capitalism and climate change.* London: Allen Lane.

Kolbert, E. (2014). *The sixth extinction: An unnatural history.* New York, NY: Henry Holt.

Lansley, S. (2012). *The cost of inequality: Why economic equality is essential for recovery.* London: Gibson Square.

Lorde, A. (1984). *The master's tools will never dismantle the master's house.* Retrieved from http://collectiveliberation.org/wpcontent/uploads/2013/01/Lorde_The_Masters_Tools.pdf

Mathiesen, K. (2016). *Why is 2016 smashing heat records?* Retrieved from http://www.theguardian.com/environment/2016/mar/04/is-el-nino-or-climate-change-behind-the-run-of-record-temperatures

Minister for Disability Issues. (2001). *The New Zealand disability strategy: Making a world of difference: Whakanui oranga.* Wellington: Ministry of Health.

Ministry of Health & University of Otago. (2006). *Decades of disparity III: Ethnic and socioeconomic inequalities in mortality, New Zealand 1981–1999.* Wellington: Ministry of Health.

Ministry of Social Development. (2016). *The social report: Te purongo oranga tangata.* Wellington: Ministry of Social Development.

Ministry of Women's Affairs. (2013). *Current thinking on primary prevention of violence against women.* Wellington: Ministry of Women's Affairs.

Monbiot, G. (2016). *Neoliberalism: The ideology at the root of all our problems.* Retrieved from http://www.theguardian.com/books/2016/apr/15/neoliberalism-ideology-problem-george-monbiot

Nairn, K., Higgins, J., & Sligo, J. (2012). *Children of Rogernomics: A neoliberal generation leaves school.* Dunedin: University of Otago Press.

Nixon, R. (2011). *Slow violence and the environmentalism of the poor*. Retrieved from http://socialtextjournal.org/slow_violence_and_the_environmentalism_of_the_poor_an_interview_with_rob_nixon/

Oldham, S. (2016). Intersections, old and new: Trade unions, worker cooperatives and the climate crisis. In D. Taylor (Ed.), *Counterfutures* (pp. 103–129). Wellington: School of Social and Cultural Studies, Victoria University of Wellington.

Olssen, M. (2002). *The neoliberal appropriation of tertiary education policy in New Zealand: Accountability, research and academic freedom*. Wellington: New Zealand Association for Research in Education.

Oreskes, N., & Conway, E. (2010). *Merchants of doubt: How a handful of scientists obscured the truth on issues from tobacco smoke to global warming*. New York, NY: Bloomsbury.

Ostry, J. D., Loungani, P., & Furceri, D. (2016). Neoliberalism: Oversold? *Finance & Development, 53*(2), 1–6. Retrieved from http://www.imf.org/external/pubs/ft/fandd/2016/06/ostry.htm

Oxfam International. (2016). *62 people own the same as half the world*. Retrieved from https://www.oxfam.org/en/pressroom/pressreleases/2016-01-18/62-people-own-same-half-world-reveals-oxfam-davos-report

Packer, G. (2013, June 19). Decline and fall: How American society unravelled. *The Guardian*. Retrieved from https://www.theguardian.com/world/2013/jun/19/decline-fall-american-society-unravelled

Palmer, G. (2016, May 19). *Preparing a written, codified constitution for New Zealand: Is there a need that can be met?* Keynote Address to a Symposium on Quasi-Constitutionality and Constitutional Statutes, Faculty of Law, Victoria University of Wellington, Wellington.

Palmer, G., & Butler, A. (2016). *Constitution Aotearoa New Zealand*. Wellington: Victoria University of Wellington Press.

Rashbrooke, M. (2015). *Wealth and New Zealand*. Wellington: Bridget Williams Books.

Saul, J. R. (2009). *The collapse of globalism and the reinvention of the world*. London: Penguin Books.

Slee, R. (2011). *The irregular school: Exclusion, schooling and inclusive education*. London: Routledge.

Smith, L. T. (2013). The future is now. In M. Rashbrooke (Ed.), *Inequality: A New Zealand crisis* (pp. 228–235). Wellington: Bridget Williams Books.

Speth, J. G. (2008). *The bridge at the end of the world: Capitalism, the environment and crossing from crisis to sustainability*. New Haven, CT: Yale University Press.

Statistics New Zealand. (2016). *Household net worth statistics*. Retrieved from http://www.stats.govt.nz/browse_for_stats/people_and_communities/Households/HouseholdNetWorthStatistics_MRYeJun15.aspx

Stern, N. (2006). *Stern review: The economics of climate change, executive summary.* Retrieved from http://webarchive.nationalarchives.gov.uk/20130129110402/ http://www.hm-treasury.gov.uk/d/Executive_Summary.pdf

Stigliz, J. E. (2003). *Globalization and its discontents.* New York, NY: W.W. Norton.

St John, S. (2014). Recalibrating New Zealand. In Tom Rennie (Ed.), *The Piketty phenomenon: New Zealand perspectives* (pp. 144–154). Wellington: Bridget Williams Books.

The Catholic Church in Aotearoa New Zealand. (2010). *The treaty of Waitangi.* Retrieved from http://www.catholic.org.nz/our-story/dsp-default.cfm?loadref=42

Treasury. (2015). *The thirty year New Zealand infrastructure plan 2015.* Retrieved from http://www.infrastructure.govt.nz/plan/2015/nip-aug15.pdf

UNICEF. (2016). *The state of the world's children 2016: A fair chance for every child.* New York, NY: UNICEF.

United Nations. (1993). *Strategies for confronting domestic violence: A resource manual.* New York, NY: United Nations.

Wilkinson, R., & Pickett, K. (2009). *The spirit level: Why more equal societies almost always do better.* London: Allen Lane.

Women's Refuge. (2016). *Statistical report 2014–2015.* Retrieved from https://womensrefuge.org.nz/wp-content/uploads/2015/11/Domestic-violence-statistics-NZ.pdf

Wylie, C. (2012). *Vital connections: Why we need more than self-managing schools.* Wellington: New Zealand Council for Educational Research.

PART 1

Participation – Belonging in Action

CHAPTER 3

Inclusion and Autism
Belonging

Marie Turner

1 Introduction

Children with an autism spectrum disorder are being enrolled at their local schools in preference to more specialised schools. School communities are progressing toward being inclusive and are meeting the diverse needs of their students who are on the autism spectrum. How they are meeting these needs and developing a community where children belong in these local schools will be the focus of my research. I have a strong connection with both children and adults with autism through my personal and professional experiences. I grew up with a brother on the autism spectrum, then became a teacher in an autism-specific special school and transitioned many children into their local school communities. My brother, his peers and the students I have had the pleasure of teaching, have provided me with experiences from different perspectives. This chapter will provide an overture of my research, exploring the experiences of myself as a sibling and teacher, as well as colleagues, who include children with autism in the classroom. It is through these lenses that I explore the concepts of inclusion and belonging, using the ethnographic approach of story-telling (Clandinin & Caine, 2013).

This chapter is informed by a series of conversations amongst supervisors and myself. Thus we each contribute a lens and perspective but the overall narrative belongs to me, Marie.

2 Family

Witnessing the experience of my brother has helped me understand the complexities of the autistic condition for nearly 50 years. According to my mother, Daniel was a very difficult baby. He refused to breastfeed, did not like wearing clothing and frequently displayed tantrums. Mum struggled to toilet train him and he did not speak. The doctors could not explain why he presented in this way, and blamed her parenting for Daniel's unusual behaviour.

My parents appeared unable to connect with my brother yet, for some reason, I could engage and interact with him. This pattern of connection has continued well into adulthood where there is now a great divide between my brother and I, and a third sibling and parents (Laing, 1971). Daniel and I live in Melbourne whilst the other members of this 'family' remain in Perth, with little or no contact. The original family unit crumbled, yet the sense of belonging between my brother and I strengthened – you and me against the world.

I have vivid memories of imitating Daniel and seeing him smile back at me in recognition, and being able to get him to copy me. Muller (2009) claims that some crucial features of Lacan's "mirror stage" include creating identity and forming relationships (p. 223). The mirror stage, originating from Lacan, refers to the moment of self-recognition by the infant aged twelve to eighteen months. It is the moment at which I realise the hand in the mirror is *my* hand. It is also when we come to understand that we can make meaning with our bodies and that others can interpret our movements. In the case of Daniel, there seemed to be some sense of alienation from the image and yet we experienced some sense of connection.

Daniel's experience of the world seemed to be different from other children. He was not interested in typical children's toys. He preferred to play with running water, spinning objects such as wheels and vinyl records and hammering nails into wood. He was quite the escape artist, being able to climb through the bathroom window to escape the house in a nanosecond. He was often found running around the neighbourhood naked, swapping sprinklers between houses or sitting under trucks at the nearby intersection, waiting to watch the wheels go round. He had a limited awareness of danger and it was usually my job to retrieve him. In this sense, I felt I somehow shared Daniel's experience of autism in a profound way. I was different just like Daniel. I was as separate from the world as Daniel because I was his carer and protector from a very young age.

He screamed a lot and was physically aggressive. It was usually because he did not get what he wanted or if I interrupted his activities. I remember many occasions being hit on the head with a hammer or having the hose turned on me when I tried to bring him in for dinner. I was literally experiencing physical symptoms as a result of his condition. His trauma had become mine and the separation of the two seemed impossible.

When Daniel was about five, he began having epileptic seizures and was admitted to hospital. A visiting doctor from Switzerland suggested that Daniel might have autism and subsequent assessments confirmed the diagnosis. It was 1971 and Daniel was one of the first in Western Australia to receive a diagnosis of autism. Our father did not accept the professional opinions of the doctor and often said that Daniel was being naughty and strong-willed. Very little was known about the condition at the time or about intervention and support. Daniel was subjected to violent outbursts by his father, which was spurred on by his lack of tolerance and acceptance of both the diagnosis and of Daniel's behaviour.

3   School

Daniel attended my local primary school and I was his minder. He did not speak and had difficulty attending when I was not sitting next to him. His final day at my school was quite memorable. He was seven years old. It was early in the day and he had climbed through the venetian blinds and out of the classroom window. He rearranged the sprinkler pipes on the school oval and blew up the school's reticulation system. Daniel later attended a special education class at an independent boys school. The cage he was in during his time in a mainstream school, began to open as he learned the power of using words and began to talk. He remained at this school until the end of year ten where he transitioned to a work skills program and later, employment.

In 2000 Daniel moved to Melbourne to live with me. He was offered a position packing boxes at a registered disability supported workplace. In 2011 he moved into supported housing and lives with five other men who have a range of disabilities and a roster of paid carers. Daniel is learning to play the clarinet and has a girlfriend who lives in a supported house nearby. A strong sense of belonging for Daniel was generated through his relationship with me as his sister, in his own living space and workplace, a social network including his girlfriend and his community. The label of autism provides a framework for understanding the difficulties and the beneficial interventions that can be put in place to alleviate some of the symptoms (Norwich & Lewis, 2007). However, Daniel's sense of belonging and his ability to create his own pathway highlight the potential within us all when we question the assumptions inherent in a diagnosis through our thoughts, actions and lifestyle.

The experiences of living with my brother have influenced my perceptions of people with different abilities. He is and always will be my brother who has amazing gifts and aspects of daily life where he needs support. When I look at my students, I see their amazing gifts and aspects of their life that need additional support and it is from this perspective that I have embarked on this journey of exploring inclusive education and creating a sense of belonging for children with autism. The possibilities seem endless.

4 Belonging

My younger brother and I had a close relationship growing up together and this has continued to develop as adults. There is a powerful sense of belonging between us through shared relationships, experiences, interests and places. Wood and Black (2016) created a diagram (Figure 3.1) that represents the concept of belonging and the importance of relationships, spaces and feelings in developing a sense of belonging. All three areas intercept at the core of self and simultaneously interact with each other, creating a sense of community. Wright (2014) refers to places and communities that contribute to being and feeling human. There is symmetry between experiencing a sense of belonging and the need for educational inclusion for children with disabilities.

A tension exists between the need to provide a place of belonging for people with different abilities in the form of special schools and the somewhat contemporary notion of inclusive classrooms (Norwich, 2014). Through my personal experience and observations, a special school provided Daniel with the skills and environment that allowed him to interact with others. He had a physical place where he connected to his peers, teachers and the school community. These skills included learning to talk and remaining clothed. Further to this, his relationships with others and his own feeling of belonging

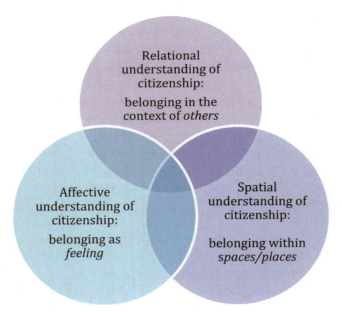

FIGURE 3.1   Belonging (from Wood & Black, 2016, reproduced with permission)

helped him regulate his behaviour in a socially acceptable manner. Within this space of a special education classroom his peers, who were also socially challenged by normative assumptions about being and belonging, accepted him. His teachers were able to bring out his strengths and interests. Even now, Daniel reminisces fondly of his time in this class and his teachers. Daniel went on school camps with his peers and teachers, enjoyed music and gymnastics at school and received achievement certificates for his efforts in class. He experienced a sense of belonging through shared experiences with his peers, the teachers that created the space where he felt safe and was nurtured.

5 Teacher

As a teacher within the special education sector, I have seen students with a diagnosis of autism transform once they have learned the power of communication and the pleasure of developing friendships based on shared interests. A sense of belonging; physical, social and feelings have been co-created through their interactions with each other and with staff (Wood & Black, 2016). The students became part of a learning space that developed over the school year.

Within this particular specialized setting, communication and social skills are taught explicitly by specialist teachers, within a small class of six to eight children, the intention being to gradually increase the group size where skills can be generalized. When most children arrive in my class they have very little functional language. The communicative behaviours displayed by many include pointing, screaming or just grabbing an item that they want. Students learn how to request items, either verbally or with a communication device, take turns and share toys (Twachtman-Cullen, 2008). These skills provide the foundations for further learning, often through play activities. The ultimate aim for students is to transition to their local schools after one to two years, where they are welcomed and have the opportunity to remain engaged in learning and their community.

6 Inclusion in Education

The move toward inclusive education has been driven by United Nations policy and social reforms (Barton, 2003; Goodley, 2007). 'Inclusive education' is a term used in schools to describe learning that provides a quality education for all learners of all abilities (Cambridge-Johnson, Hunter-Johnson, & Newton,

2014; Humphrey & Symes, 2013). The term emerged from a change in the law in United States Congress in 1975, which allowed all children to receive free public education in the "least restrictive environment" (Lipsky & Gartner, 1998; Mastropieri & Scruggs, 2000) and became known as the *Individuals with Disabilities Education Act* (IDEA). This law was the beginning of the breaking down of boundaries for children with disabilities and also the catalyst for greater inclusive practices within school communities.

In the state of Victoria, all schools are required to meet the Disability Standards for Education 2005 under Section 32 of the Disabilities Act 1992 (DEECD, 2015). These standards provide a framework for schools to develop a more inclusive community. Schools are required to modify or adapt their programs and environments to ensure that students with disabilities, including the disability label of autism, are able to participate in the same way as their peers. Modifications may include using visual cues, breaking down tasks into smaller chunks, computer equipment and software, adapting the curriculum and methods of assessment. These provisions aim to maximize the learning outcomes and experiences for people with disabilities in Victorian schools.

7 Understanding Some Characteristics of Autism

Autism Spectrum Condition (ASC) is a complex, puzzling, lifelong and grossly misunderstood neurological disorder (Attwood, 1998, 2007; Barton, Robins, Jashar, Brennan, & Fein, 2013; Ruzich et al., 2016). Children with autism become adults with autism. The condition manifests differently in each person with a range of challenges in communication, social skills, sensory processing and behavioural implications. Each experience of autism is unique and we cannot draw conclusions about the condition through our observations of one person, we can only add to the narrative or testimonial evidence on the subject (Wing, Gould, & Gillberg, 2011). Teachers are often not able to recognize or identify appropriate learning goals without having an understanding of the complex challenges faced by children on the spectrum. A teacher's understanding of autism and how the condition affects learning can greatly improve a child's learning outcomes and progressive independence.

Children and young people with a diagnosis of autism (ASC) typically have difficulty with expressive (speaking) and receptive (listening) communication (Twachtman-Cullen, 2008). Many children have difficulty developing speech. Some of my students may be verbal but lack the understanding of what others are saying, making it difficult for them to gain meaning or participate in the conversation. Some children with autism never learn to talk and use augmentative communication such as electronic communication devices to express themselves. There are also children who develop speech later and some who seem verbally precocious for their age. Often a child seems to talk incessantly about their favourite topics however this type of behaviour can be a mask for underlying comprehension difficulties, high levels of anxiety or an attempt to engage with people but not knowing what else to talk about (Baron-Cohen, 2014; Twachtman-Cullen, 2008).

Many children with autism experience difficulty engaging in social interactions. Children and adults have reported that they do not know how to begin or end a conversation (Grandin, 2011). They also tell us that they are not sure when to join in, make comments or change topics. Recognizing and interpreting body language, making eye contact, interpreting jokes or using sarcasm, some facial expressions and voice tone create a minefield of anxiety (Baron-Cohen, 2014).

Sensory stimulation can be another hurdle that children (and adults) with ASC tend to experience (Ashburner, Ziviani, & Rodger, 2008). Visual stimulation such as lighting in supermarkets, bright, coloured signs or animation can overwhelm or mesmerize someone and effectively block out any verbal directions or instructions given by a parent or carer. Noise can also impact on a child or adult on the spectrum. Sudden noise such as cheering or clapping can overwhelm a person. The response can range from slight annoyance to a child putting their hands over ears or running away from the source. Sensitivities to the environment such as smells and clothing textures can also impact on the child with autism and their ability to attend to verbal instructions, including crucial communications leading the child to safety or warning of danger. Students have a greater opportunity to experience a sense of belonging and feeling part of their classroom community when teachers take into consideration the sensory sensitivities that some students may be experiencing.

8 Autism-Specific Classroom – An Example

In 2008 I was asked to establish a classroom for children who had been referred to the school from their mainstream settings and the Royal Melbourne Children's Hospital. The students were aged between nine and twelve years of age and were too old to join the early years programs and too young to join the secondary group. These students were all displaying violent behaviour and their schools were not able to ensure their safety or those of the other classmates. None of the students had an intellectual disability, deeming them ineligible for other special school settings. The principal and educational psychologist shared their vision of an academic program combined with social skills and behavioural support.

We had the space. The focus turned to developing relationships. This was achieved through shared interests and experiences, as well as establishing ground rules for friendships – treat others with kindness and respect. During a reflective social skills activity one of the boys referred to himself as a "little genius who did not understand friendship rules". I suggested the term 'mini-Einstein'. The class identified with this and it stuck. I now refer to this group affectionately as 'mini-Einstein's' who may be described as both socially awkward and wonderfully unique.

These students had all come from mainstream primary schools where they had been suspended or expelled, withdrawn themselves or removed by parents due to concerns for their health and well-being. They had all experienced rejection, significant failure and exhibited violent outbursts. I needed to engage this group of students back into learning by developing their own sense of belonging – to the classroom, each other and to me.

This small section of the school maintained the general principles that underpinned the rest of the school and included current best practice for teaching children with autism (Mesibov & Shea, 2011). The school's philosophy and strategies for teaching children with ASC strongly adhere to Mesibov's TEACCH program. The strategies recommended by Mesibov's team include the need for highly structured learning activities for children with autism. Adhering to these recommendations, my class used consistent daily routines to provide students with predictability and provided visual schedules of classroom activities and events were made available.

The teaching team was assembled by the principal and the school's educational psychologist, and consisted of a classroom assistant and myself. There was also invaluable support from staff in the adjoining classroom, who taught students of high school age with an ASC diagnosis. Staff were rotated between both rooms to enable the development of relationships among all students and staff, while increasing consistency for the students when some staff were absent.

Our initial meeting with the boys was quite daunting. Steven (12 yrs) refused to participate and had a diagnosed eating disorder. Jeremy (9 yrs) announced that he was a compulsive liar and enjoyed controlling adults, Adam (10 yrs) described himself as an angry "bone-breaker", and Alan (9 yrs) was hyperactive and disruptive with a history of absconding. Along with their individual issues there were common factors to consider:

1. Each student had a diagnosis of being on the autism spectrum, which explained the difficulties with communication and social interactions.
2. Anger and frustration felt by not being able to articulate emotions or read social cues impacted negatively on relationships with their peers, family and teachers (Attwood, 2007).
3. When the boys attempted to interact with others, it consolidated their own self-perception of never fitting in with others.
4. Each of the boys verbalised their low opinions of themselves and presented violent behaviours, including severe verbal and physical aggression, disruptions and teasing, lying, stealing and manipulating others.

It was also difficult to establish any base-lining data to gauge where their literacy and numeracy skills were due to the group's refusal to participate in activities, possibly due to their history of failure. It quickly became very clear that refusal was a well-used strategy to minimise the negative fallout of failure, and it was easier to deal with the ridicule and punishment of removal or isolation than to attempt activities that would produce yet another failure, and re-enforce their negative self-perception.

The program aimed to engage the students, establish boundaries and increase their perceptions of themselves. It was also critical to change their understanding of what school is all about, and provide positive experiences and connectedness with staff and each other. It was clear by early interactions and observations of the boys, that there was no intellectual impairment, in fact, I believe that had they participated in an IQ test, would have been in the top 10th percentile for their ages.

Since all the boys shared the experience of being bullied, this provided a context for conversations about oneself and ones' experiences. Rules were established as a class to eliminate the potential for any further instances of bullying or aggression. We began with a large sheet of butchers' paper and some coloured marker pens. The students complained about being made to write so I offered to scribe, as the main objective was to get the students to articulate their thoughts and ideas. All comments would be acknowledged and an agreement was made to refrain from swearing. They were then very keen to participate in a class brainstorm about how they had been bullied. Many of their comments and ideas were in a negative format, for example, "I hate people yelling at me". These ideas were grouped into four categories, and a rule was made as a group, about each area. Instead of yelling, the rule became "Use an inside voice when you are in class". This chart of rules, put together by the boys, with guidance from my assistant and myself, was displayed with everyone signing their names in agreement. A 'zero tolerance' for bullying was established with the consequence of breaking the agreed rules also clearly displayed, which involved missing out on certain activities.

Research has shown that when any behavioural management program is established, the identified behaviour increases until the targeted group reach consistent boundaries (Strain, Barton, & Dunlap, 2012; Tonge, Brereton, Gray, & Einfeld, 1999). The boys did not disappoint and pulled out everything they had in an attempt to sabotage the program. However, within two weeks, the students were sitting down at the tables doing written work, speaking to each other without swearing and were mostly compliant with staff instructions. A rewards system was also introduced to help the students stay motivated to maintain the positive behaviours that had been established. The Unit had recently purchased a Nintendo Wii interactive games console, which was ideal for motivation, as all students loved opportunities to play with this new technology and receive two ticks towards their earning of Wii time.

Fatigue which ordinarily set in by the middle of the morning sessions, was noticed and questions were raised about eating and sleeping patterns. An issue was identified: the boys were skipping breakfast because they either did not get time before the bus picked them up in the mornings or just did not want to eat. Morning exercises were introduced followed by a breakfast program at school. The exercise regime included a variety of ball games, bike-riding and running. The boys quickly adapted to this routine, and also seemed to enjoy sitting around the kitchen table with cereal, toast and fresh fruit, participating in light-hearted conversations about favourite activities at home, family pets and television programs. They learnt to do their dishes and assist with making lists for weekly shopping excursions. Wright (2014) suggests that working together on a joint task increases feelings of unity within the group and ownership of the space. Activities such as breakfast and working together to clean the kitchen or prepare the shopping list provided a vehicle for positive banter and skills in negotiation, which developed a sense of community and belonging.

An education program works most effectively when students are engaged in their own learning (Prain et al., 2012). Therefore, the best activities are those based on the interests of the students. When you have an interested student, you are able to engage them in learning (Tomlinson & Imbeau, 2010). The curriculum focused on activities-based objectives, rather than objectives-based activities, and provided the foundation for learning appropriate communicative and social behaviours. Students then had the skills to enable learning curriculum content and interact positively with their peers, developing friendship groups and enhancing self-esteem, thereby increasing their sense of belonging within the class.

The fun factor was participating in science experiments and other hands-on activities. One example was when the students followed written instructions to build a ski slope as a group using cardboard, string, plasticine and craft sticks. Races were held using Lego men where the students experimented with changing the amount of ramp inclination to produce a faster speed. The boys designed and made wooden cars, clay models and battery-operated spinning Ferris wheels. An arts-based program provided the students with another avenue for self-development and creativity. Cooking meals also produced excellent results with developing independent living skills. With such an engaging focus, conversation, social skills and friendships were emerging and achievements were experienced. They showed pride in their work and were eager to show their finished product to each other and staff and discuss their ideas and methods.

9   Daily Learning

The timetable was broken up into three main sessions: being a morning, middle and afternoon. Initially the focus was on developing relationships and setting ground rules to ensure that everyone felt safe. Activities were presented and students were given choices about how they could complete the tasks.

The morning session started at 9am. Some students arrived with their parents and others were dropped off by the school's taxi. Students were encouraged to pack away their bags and electronic equipment (phones, gaming devices) and join in a ball game or bike riding. Some children came in at odd times so having an open-ended sporting game meant that they were not disadvantaged by missing out on the morning activities.

Most of the students (all boys) were on medication and did not eat breakfast before they got to school. The morning exercises provided an opportunity for staff to bond with the students and the energy used piqued their appetites. We offered breakfast each morning, which usually consisted of cereals, toast and fruit. On Fridays we made pancakes. We all prepared and ate breakfast then cleaned up together. The breakfast program engaged the students and gave us an opportunity to talk around the breakfast table without the power imbalance of the teacher/student relationship. Relationships between the students and staff developed most during these moments of camaraderie, as we shared our thoughts and ideas on a more personal level.

These students were willing to learn but did not always seem to have a positive attitude when presented with new tasks. However, within the space of about four weeks each of the students were actively engaged in academic learning. Work was structured and routines were established. Students were able to take mini "movement" breaks and seek assistance at any time. However, there was an understanding that all work needed to be completed before they had their morning tea, lunch breaks or playtime.

The middle session was focused on social interactions within the school and community excursions. We spent a lot of time talking and role-playing different social scenarios and discussing responses to behaviours such as name-calling, teasing and excluding people from an activity. We also enjoyed going to a basketball court at a local YMCA, making music at the Arts Centre in Melbourne and going on interest-based excursions. The afternoon session was divided into two parts with structured relaxation time then leisure activities. We did yoga or guided relaxation, colouring, drawing or construction.

Positive behaviour re-inforcers that recognize and encourage constructive behaviours have been very successful in my experience. The students earned ticks on a chart displayed in the room. When students were caught following rules, organizing and completing work tasks or demonstrating friendship skills they were awarded ticks. These accumulated in order for the students to purchase special privileges such as choosing excursions, extra computer time and opportunities to play on the Nintendo Wii. Students were also given verbal praise, which initially they found hard to accept, high 5's, and free time when work was completed early.

Staff and students worked closely together with the intention of getting to know them as much as possible. We found out about students' interests, family life, motivators and triggers for meltdowns. All this information provided a profile of each student in order to develop a program that would achieve the best learning outcomes. This is particularly important when there has been a history of opposition, violent aggression towards staff and other anti-social behaviour. Staff needed to be alert to potential triggers and diffuse the situation. If a situation arose that continually caused inappropriate responses, staff analyzed the behaviour patterns, and developed strategies as a team.

Physical exercise was a daily preventative measure. When students arrived each morning, they were instructed to run laps, ride bikes, play football and other ball games. If students were restless during work sessions they could take themselves off for a run or walk around the school playground. This did not take the place of the work required, which needed to be completed without negotiation. However, this mental and physical break allowed students to process issues causing anxiety and eventually got to a point where they could ask for assistance. How work was to be completed could then be negotiated.

Emotional health and anger management were major components of the program. Daily opportunities to hone all the 'prickles', dealing with social situations as they arose, were critical learning moments. Issues were usually worked through as they occurred, and usually it was better to let the emotions cool before addressing concerns. Structured social activities were facilitated daily, as these skills needed to be taught explicitly to students with autism, and were often disguised as games, birthday parties and excursions.

Towards the end of their second year in this classroom, each student was transitioned into a different local school with their same-aged peers. Whilst we may believe in the idea of inclusion, in practice, transitions can often be a difficult process for all concerned. Many of the families have kept in contact and report that they are generally doing well. The continued engagement of these students in their local schools may be attributed to a range of factors, which will become evident through my research.

10 Conclusion

The aim of this chapter has been to provide an insight into the background, the prologue to my research, which involves an exploration of teachers' experiences including students with autism in their classroom communities. More specifically, how schools are engaged with my 'mini-Einsteins'. The experiences described above and my PhD journey, will inform the gap in research on teacher success with students with a diagnosis of autism. The personal experiences with my brother and the students who I have taught, have provided unique insights into the challenges and opportunities faced daily. Understanding some of the characteristics of autism, such as difficulties with communication and social skills, provide teachers with some indicators in how best to orchestrate learning, create inclusive classrooms and improve learning outcomes. In my experience, co-constructing relationships between all members of the classroom and school community have been integral in developing a sense of belonging. The transformations of these students, who started with so many prickles and became 'mini-Einsteins' illustrate the potential in each of us when we feel we belong; to a place, to each other and to a community.

Acknowledgements

Pseudonyms have been used to protect the identities of all the students.

I would like to thank and acknowledge the support and guidance of my supervisors Dr Gwen Gilmore and Dr Scott Welsh in writing this chapter.

References

Ashburner, J., Ziviani, J., & Rodger, S. (2008). Sensory processing and classroom emotional, behavioral, and educational outcomes in children with autism spectrum disorder. *American Journal of Occupational Therapy, 62*(5), 564–573. Retrieved from http://o-search.ebscohost.com.library.vu.edu.au/login.aspx?direct=true&db=mnh&AN=18826017&site=eds-live

Attwood, A. (1998). *Asperger's syndrome: A guide for parents and professionals.* London: Jessica Kingsley Publishers.

Attwood, A. (2007). *The complete guide to aspergers syndrome.* London: Jessica Kingsley Publishers.

Baron-Cohen, S. (2014). *Handbook of autism and anxiety* (T. E. Davis, S. W. White, & T. H. Ollendick Eds.). Louisiana: Springer International Publishing.

Barton, L. (2003). *Inclusive-education: A basis for hope and discourse of delusion.* Paper presented at the 100 Years in Education, London.

Barton, M. L., Robins, D. L., Jashar, D., Brennan, L., & Fein, D. (2013). Sensitivity and specificity of proposed dsm-5 criteria for autism spectrum disorder in toddlers. *Journal of Autism and Developmental Disorders, 43*(5), 1184–1195. doi:10.1007/s10803-013-1817-8

Cambridge-Johnson, J., Hunter-Johnson, Y., & Newton, N. G. L. (2014). Breaking the silence of mainstream teachers attitude towards inclusive education in the Bahamas: High school teachers' perceptions. *The Qualitative Report, 19*(42), 1–20. Retrieved from http://nsuworks.nova.edu/cgi/viewcontent.cgi?article=1099&context=tqr

Clandinin, D. J., & Caine, V. (2013). Narrative inquiry. In A. Trainor & E. Graue (Eds.), *Reviewing qualitative research in the social sciences* (pp. 166–179). New York, NY: Routledge.

DEECD. (2015). *Program for students with disabilities: Guidelines for schools 2016.* Retrieved from http://www.education.vic.gov.au/school/principals/spag/curriculum/Pages/disabilities.aspx

Goodley, D. (2007). Towards socially just pedagogies: Deleuzoguattarian critical disability studies. *International Journal of Inclusive Education, 11*(3), 317–334. doi:10.1080/13603110701238769

Grandin, T. (2011). *The way I see it.* Arlington, TX: Future Horizons.

Humphrey, N., & Symes, W. (2013). Inclusive education for pupils with autistic spectrum disorders in secondary mainstream schools: Teacher attitudes, experience and knowledge. *International Journal of Inclusive Education, 17*(1), 32–46. doi:10.1080/13603116.2011.580462

Laing, R. (1971). *The politics of the family, and other essays* (Vol. 5). New York, NY: Vintage Books.

Lipsky, D. K., & Gartner, A. (1998). Taking inclusion into the future. *Educational Leadership, 56*, 78–81. Retrieved from https://eric.ed.gov/?id=EJ573484

Mastropieri, M. A., & Scruggs, T. E. (2000). *The inclusive classroom: Strategies for effective instruction* (A. C. Davis, Ed.). Columbus, OH: Prentice Hall.

Mesibov, G. B., & Shea, V. (2011). Evidence-based practices and autism. *Autism, 15*, 114–133. doi:10.1177/1362361309348070

Muller, J. (2009). Lacan's mirror stage. *Psychoanalytic Inquiry, 5*(2), 233–252. doi:10.1080/07351698509533586

Norwich, B. (2014). Recognising value tensions that underlie problems in inclusive education. *Cambridge Journal of Education, 44*(4), 495–510. doi:10.1080/0305764x.2014.963027

Norwich, B., & Lewis, A. (2007). How specialized is teaching children with disabilities and difficulties? *Journal of Curriculum Studies, 39*(2), 127–150. doi:10.1080/00220270601161667

Prain, V., Cox, P., Deed, C., Dorman, J., Edwards, D., Farrelly, C., Keeffe, M., Lovejoy, V., Mow, L., Sellings, P., Waldrip, B., & Yager, Z. (2012). Personalised learning: Lessons to be learnt. *British Educational Research Journal, 39*(4), 654–676. doi:10.1080/01411926.2012.669747

Ruzich, E., Allison, C., Smith, P., Ring, H., Auyeung, B., & Baron-Cohen, S. (2016). The autism-spectrum quotient in siblings of people with autism. *Autism Research, 9*(10), 1114. doi:10.1002/aur.1651

Strain, P. S., Barton, E. E., & Dunlap, G. (2012). Lessons learned about the utility of social validity. *Education and Treatment of Children, 35*(2), 183–200. doi:10.1353/etc.2012.0007

Tomlinson, C. A., & Imbeau, M. B. (2010). *Leading and managing a differentiated classroom*. Alexandria, VA: ASCD Publications.

Tonge, B. J., Brereton, A. V., Gray, K. M., & Einfeld, S. L. (1999). Behavioural and emotional disturbance in high-functioning autism and asperger syndrome. *Autism, 3*(2), 117–130. doi:10.1177/1362361399003002003

Twachtman-Cullen, D. (2008). Symbolic communication: Common pathways and points of departure. In K. Dunn Buron & P. Wolfberg (Eds.), *Learners on the spectrum preparing highly qualified educators*. Shawnee Mission, KS: Autism Aspergers Publishing.

Wing, L., Gould, J., & Gillberg, C. (2011). Autism spectrum disorders in the dsm-v: Better or worse than the dsm-iv? *Research in Developmental Disabilities, 32*(2), 768–773. doi:10.1016/j.ridd.2010.11.003

Wood, B. E., & Black, R. (2016). *Spatial, relational and affective understandings of citizenship and belonging for young people today: Towards a new conceptual framework*. Paper presented at the Interrogating Belonging in Education, Deakin University, Melbourne, Australia.

Wright, S. (2014). More-than-human, emergent belongings: A weak theory approach. *Progress in Human Geography, 39*(4), 391–411. doi:10.1177/0309132514537132

CHAPTER 4

Theory Circles, Inclusion and the PhD Student

Be Pannell, Julie White and Fiona Henderson

1   Introduction

In this chapter, the concept of inclusive education is applied to PhD students who are faced with the task of completing complex research within academic environments that are increasingly time limited and managed. To attend to such a task, we reconsider three aspects of this problem, namely; the notion of inclusion, the formation of a scholarly identity, and the intellectual environment in which both occur. We address these problems by examining recent trends to think with theory within qualitative research projects, and demonstrate how theory can be constructively used to broaden the concept of inclusive education and research practices. Furthermore, this chapter will consider how post structural theories trouble the formation of static scholarly identities by challenging assumptions behind the isolated, independent subject, and instead contextualise PhD scholarship within an environment of constant change and becoming. In concluding this chapter, we demonstrate how inclusive PhD education works in practice by describing the 2016 'Queen Street Project' at The Victoria Institute, Victoria University. In this project students were included in a supportive supervision and training program, where post structural theories were put to work to both enhance a sense of belonging in the group and to foster academic readiness. This supported the students to feel better equipped to undertake the complex work of learning to think with, and apply theory to their own research projects.

2   Doctoral Students and Inclusion

This chapter connects doctoral candidates to inclusion and theory and considers the concept of belonging to the academy. Inclusion is not limited to mainstream schooling for children with impairments, although this remains part of the discourse, PhD students do not usually feature in discussions of inclusive education. Inclusion can also refer to those from stigmatised backgrounds or any group who are marginalised, as observed by many scholars, including the recent book by Harwood, Hickey-Moody, McMahon, and O'Shea (2016).

With academic institutions undergoing massification over the past twenty years, increasing numbers of students are accepted into universities to meet government targets, which is generally accepted as a positive move. However, simply enrolling students without adequately accommodating them presents new problems. As Slee (2011) reminds us, enrolment in an educational institution does not constitute inclusion.

The high fees paid by international students and the financial rewards paid to universities for timely completions of doctoral students have become necessary for underfunded universities, but have brought new expectations of both students and their supervisors. Older styles of supervision such as a laissez-faire approach is no longer seen as adequate, but micromanaging a hurried candidature is not satisfactory either. What kind of supervision is appropriate and who makes decisions about these issues is of particular interest here. As the grip of audit culture has become firm and universities have become increasingly managed, the process of supervision and PhD development has experienced increasing surveillance mechanisms such as compulsory PhD supervision courses, regular progress reports and the use of supervisory panels. These technologies are not necessarily conducive to thoughtful and original contributions to knowledge. Nor do they serve to improve educational inclusion of students from diverse backgrounds. To address this problem, this chapter considers how PhD candidature might be viewed in the light of post structural theories that trouble the notion of the subject of inclusion, and secondly reconceptualise the intellectual environment in which research methodologies are based.

3   The Managed University and Doctoral Candidates

As universities have increasingly become managed (Utley, 2001; Shore, 2010), tangible financial income tends to dominate those traditional measures of quality such as scholarly disciplinary esteem and public intellectual work (White, 2015). What counts as worthwhile doctoral knowledge and how that knowledge might be reproduced and represented has been troubled in relation to the examination process (Devos & Somerville, 2012) and the effect of audit culture on the supervisory relationship in higher education (Cribb & Gewirtz, 2006; Atkinson, Delamont, & Parry, 2000). PhD students have become positioned and perceived differently from the valued colleagues who have the most recent knowledge, as they once were. Regarding both local and international PhD candidates as 'timely units of completion' and a valuable source of university income, constrains both the students *and* their supervisors who have explicit pressure from their managers to ensure these timely completions. Becoming a researcher involves much more than acquiring new skills and knowledge, requiring instead the development and taking up of new identities, which is a complex and long-term process (White, 2015; Devos, 2005; Beck & Young, 2005). Peterson (2007) also asserts that supervision of PhD students involves complex 'category boundary work' as students construct their academic identities, while attempting to learn how to 'get it right' (p. 479).

How scholarly identities are constructed and performed depends upon culture, environment and institutional expectations of the department and university where the PhD is undertaken (White, 2012). When these environments increase performative measures and time constraints, the complexity of a PhD thesis as a substantial and considered contribution to knowledge is under threat of being untheorized and contributing little to what is already known.

In addition to the intellectual tradition of each faculty and supervisor, the PhD candidate often brings many assumptions to the research project related to the PhD structure, which produces thinking that follows the conventional chapter sequence of introduction, literature review, methodology, findings, discussion and conclusion (Kamler & Thomson, 2006, p. 84). This is also influenced by PhD 'how-to' manuals that 'concentrate on the mechanical and the predictable, thus making the PhD project appear straightforward', leaving the student unable to address the 'complex endeavours' of academic work (White, 2013, p. 187). Students are also prone to biases towards certain research methodologies, often without understanding the theoretical (epistemological) assumptions behind them. Furthermore, they bring unquestioned ontological assumptions, such as cultural and philosophical interpretations and failing to recognise the implicit presumption of what it means to be a subject, what it means to use the phrase "I", as in "I, the researcher, considered this research question".

One of the central aims of the Queen Street Project was to introduce students to theories that challenge their conventional ways of thinking, so that education could be more inclusive of a range of students who had little exposure to newer theories and so the absent, inclusive and scholarly learning environment could be developed and fostered. As explained below, this twofold approach of troubling inclusive education both theoretically and practically, attempts to merge theoretical doctoral level reading and thinking with a greater sense of belonging for PhD candidates. In the following section, the influence of post structural theory on doctoral level thinking and identity creation is mapped. Then we address how this extends the concept of inclusion within the academy. Finally, how the learning environment of the Queen Street project creates a supportive supervisory context for inclusion and belonging is outlined.

4 Post Structural Theory

Recent theoretical trends in qualitative research include post modernism, post structuralism and post humanism. These 'posts' are part of a broader historical and philosophical movement where static assumptions around knowledge formation, objectivity, logic and truth (epistemology), subjectivity, identity and being (ontology), as well as power and agency are all challenged and deconstructed. As Whitburn (2016) explains, 'post-structural methodologies change the construction of knowledge – casting doubt on universal truths, flattening ontology, eschewing objectivism and bringing representation into question' (p. 120). One of the characteristics of these 'posts' is firstly the reversal of the dominance of epistemology over ontology, and secondly the dismantling of clear boundaries between the two (St. Pierre, 2013).

One of the most popular post structural philosophers is Gilles Deleuze, whose work has inspired a plethora of books on topics ranging from education and research, to politics and activism, to literature and performance art. His theories are popular as they mobilise the activity of thinking itself, where thought no longer needs to follow linear, binary, representational logic, and theories of knowledge production are secondary to an ontological model of the world that is in a state of constant flux, change and becoming. For Deleuze (1995) thinking is not so much about critique, which references one idea in relation to another while remaining bounded within the same conceptual confines, but rather it is about generating new ideas, following novel 'lines of flight', taking thought along entirely different trajectories. As such the concepts of truth and validity are no longer based on reference to some abstract normalised ideal, but rather for Deleuze, a concept is valid if it is useful, and so he asks not if something is true, but rather the more demanding question: 'Does it work, and how does it work?' (1995, p. 8).

In addition, Deleuze and other post structural theorists challenge ontological and cultural assumptions of an independent, autonomous humanist subject, and instead, the subject is conceptualised as socially, culturally and discursively constructed within an ever changing environment, as will be addressed below. Shildrick (2012) explains further that post structural thinking deconstructs the binaries between oneself and others, which challenges the idea of normalcy and posits the self as 'always embodied, dependent on others, unsettled, and always in process' (p. 37).

Another radical implication of this ontological shift is to no longer privilege the interiority of a separate, thinking subject, and instead open the subject up to the forces of the outside such as time, space, other human subjects and also other non-human subjects (animals, forces of nature etc.). As a result, post structural theories re-write notions such as power, where for example, Foucault (1982) examines the power discourses *between* the individual and State or individual and environment, in contrast to the idea of one entity having power *over* another. Miller (2005) explains the implications of this in relation to research practices:

> Imagine a 'structuralist' at work in research. Firstly he (they mostly were) would collect data, as speech, documents, etc. Next, he might look for structural properties suggested by the data. Then he would decide what sorts of theories (psychological, anthropological, linguistic, etc.) addressed his purposes in collecting such data...Now for the poststructuralist. She will also collect data. But the process is a little different. There is a similar eye on what the subjects are saying, writing, doing. But the other eye, a cock-eye, is on what is not said, what discourses make it impossible to say, what practical or theoretical logics hide away from sight. The interest here, following Foucault, is in how power is intrinsically present in all forms of knowledge. (p. 313)

5   Thinking with theory

As considered elsewhere (White, 2015), the use of theory in research can be sidestepped in contract research where those commissioning projects require straightforward and accessible results. Contract research, particularly for governments, is preferred in uncomplicated, definitive forms, such as survey results. Qualitative research has become increasingly complex, which can lead to difficulty in relation to contract research. The challenge for the contemporary qualitative researcher might be considered alongside equivalent issues for the novelist or artist. Is critical or popular acclaim of greater value? Is having your work valued by international peers, who read your articles in prestigious journals important? Or does bringing contract research money into your university have greater importance? It's a dilemma most researchers face at some point and unfortunately those researchers who focus on government contract dollars seem to be prized within institutions, despite other costs such as becoming (professionally) co-opted by government or corporations (see Rizvi, 2008; Shore, 2010).

The problem with removing theoretical aspects from research projects is, when thinking and researching, 'we always bring tradition with us into the new, and it is very difficult to think outside our training, which, in spite of our best efforts, normalizes our thinking and doing' (Lather & St. Pierre, 2013, p. 630). Post structural and post qualitative scholars respond to this dilemma by attempting to interrupt 'habits of thought' (McCoy, 2012, p. 766) so as to experiment with ways to think 'the world differently' (St. Pierre, 2013, p. 652). Thus post structural and post qualitative theories begin by acknowledging the theoretical assumptions that underpin research methodologies, by reconceptualising the intellectual milieu in which research practices occur. For Lather and St. Pierre (2013) this means drawing attention to some unquestioned assumptions and attachments behind qualitative epistemologies so that research practices can 'become sharper' and thus more effective (p. 631). In particular, post structural theories begin with a study of ontology and epistemology, prior to the use of research methodologies, as St. Pierre argues in a recent interview (Guttorm, Hohti, & Paakkari, 2015). Further, students are exhorted to question theories behind research practices, as they are usually normalised and dominant discourses such as neoliberalism, which she argues is 'racist, sexist, classist, and so on' (p. 15).

The importance of theory in contemporary qualitative research is also addressed by Jackson and Mazzei (2012), who make the strong assertion that to challenge dominant practices in much traditional and contemporary qualitative research, theoretical assumptions must be included. In addition, thinking with theory becomes a useful methodological approach itself, as they demonstrate by reading one piece of interview data via different theoretical perspectives. In this way Jackson and Mazzei offer a novel and substantial contribution to knowledge in the qualitative research field. This new perspective may be uncomfortable, but nevertheless provokes thought and leads to new practices and understandings, as they explain:

> qualitative data interpretation and analysis does not happen via mechanistic coding, reducing data to themes, and writing up transparent narratives that do little to critique the complexities of social life; such simplistic approaches preclude dense and multi-layered treatment of data. Furthermore, we challenge simplistic treatments of data and data analysis in qualitative research that…reduce complicated and conflicting voices and data to thematic "chunks" that can be interpreted free of context and circumstance. (pp. vii–viii)

Thinking with theory as a methodological approach is complex and difficult. MacLure (2010) argues that theory should 'get in the way', that it can and should offend, disrupt and deconstruct habitual modes of thinking and practicing, to deconstruct the cliché and 'open new possibilities for thinking and doing' (p. 277). Post structural theory in particular has the capacity to offend: nothing is fixed, there's no transcendent ideal, no abstract notion of truth or simplistic notions on which to rest. Thinking with theory in research employs Foucault's (1974) proposal that his theoretical contribution provides us with tools to assist with thinking about other or new concepts. As he explains: 'I would like my books to be a kind of tool box which others can rummage through to find a tool which they can use however they wish in their own area...I would like [my work] to be useful to an educator, a warden, a magistrate, a conscientious objector. I don't write for an audience, I write for users, not readers' (p. 523, cited in O'Farrell, 2005, p. 50).

The challenge for students learning to think in this manner, is that theoretical tools, such as Foucault's notion of discursive power cannot be applied in the same manner as a research methodology, and so research gets messy, complicated and mangled (Jackson, 2013, p. 741). As a result, students who work with contemporary theory develop the capacity to work with more sophisticated and overlapping concepts that often have no clear outcome. Braidotti (2010) concedes that this can test our 'methodological stamina' (p. 28) as this type of research is always 'incomplete' and always in the process of 'becoming' (Deleuze, 1997, p. 225).

6   Post Structural Theories and the Subject

While post structural theories challenge habituated modes of thinking, and standard research methodologies, these theories make the greatest impact as part of the recent 'ontological turn', where 'the "I" no longer centers inquiry' (St. Pierre, p. 53). This conceptual shift entails asking questions about subjectivity (ontology), prior to any consideration of epistemologies or methodologies, which makes post structural research 'inherently ontological' (Whitburn, 2016, p. 120). The implications of this ontological turn are far reaching, with subjectivity being 'the linchpin that...topples every other supposed stable referent' (St. Pierre, 2009, p. 229). This led St Pierre to question:

> What would it mean for relations if they did not involve pre-existent, self-contained individuals identifying and interacting with each other within the structure of some a priori space/time but, instead, were an individuation that was always starting up again in the middle of a

different temporality, in new assemblages, never fully constituted, fluid, a flow meeting other flows? (2004, pp. 290–291)

As post structural theories define the world as being in a state of change, flux and becoming, so too, the individual subject, student, or researcher is similarly defined as mutable, dynamic and in flux. The 'posts' articulate a world where the isolated, individual subject gives way to a view where the interior thinking of the individual is no longer separate to the external material world of others, forces and encounters.

Not only is thought and materiality enfolded and dynamic, so too is the human and environment, where post human theories challenge the anthropocentricism or human centred modes of thinking that dominate humanist research models. According to Lather and St. Pierre (2013), enfolding the interior thinking subject with the external materiality of the world, 'renders humanist qualitative research as we know it unthinkable' (p. 631), because there is no longer a separate researcher standing outside the research project, objectively analysing research data, the research practice becomes an experiment with differing forms of knowledge production. St. Pierre asserts that humanist research models assume that 'the researcher is not always already in the middle of everything, in the middle of many different studies that have already begun that she might continue' (Guttorm et al., 2015, p. 15).

As a result, post structural theories radically challenge Rose's (1997) concept of situated knowledges, which presumes a static, reflexive subject whose situated position remains untouched by the research process. Post structural theories instead situate the researcher within a complex, ever-changing environment, where each encounter with research data such as interviews, changes both the researcher and the researched. In enfolding subjectivity and knowledge production (ontology and epistemology), Barad (2007) argues, this also entails enfolding agency and ethics, which she articulates in the term 'ethico-onto-epistemology' (p. 409, note 10). St. Pierre (2013) explains that 'we are not separate from the world. Being in every sense is entangled, connected, indefinite, impersonal, shifting into different multiplicities and assemblages' (p. 653).

This ontological turn describes a mode of subjectivity that is enfolded, embedded, dynamic and mutable, and has radical implications for not only research practices and methodologies, but also for theorising about the subject of a research project, and therefore troubling such notions as 'validity', 'data', 'voice', and 'reflexivity' (St. Pierre, 2011a, p. 613). Furthermore, as Whitburn (2016) explains, questioning qualitative research practices also means that 'the lines between method and methodology are blurred' (p. 118).

Post structural and post qualitative research theories and practices are only just being mobilised and put to work in areas such as the new materialisms, post humanism and feminism, and disciplines such as ecology, education and so on. For Shildrick (2012), these theories offer 'a newly productive way of thinking that has significant material application' (p. 31), and students are introduced to more complex ways of conceptualising their own research question and practices. John Law (2004) warned against the error of methodological simplicity: 'If the world is complex and messy, then at least some of the time we're going to have to give up on simplicities' (p. 2).

7 Troubling Inclusion

So far in this chapter, we have seen how post structural theories reverse the dominance of epistemology or methodology over ontology, and also describe an ontological mode of becoming that is fluid and dynamic, where the individual subject is decentred and embedded in research practices. A further implication of the 'posts' and their deconstruction of subjectivity is that it re-writes the notion of student identity, and thus adds to the arguments that seek to trouble inclusion.

In this chapter, the notion of inclusion is broadened to consider the problem of the inclusive education for PhD students. As outlined, post structural theories that challenge habituated notions of the subject, re-write many assumptions behind standard models of inclusion (Whitburn, 2016, p. 117). Yet rather than a call for students to be included within the managed university, we want to trouble the notion of inclusion by turning to Elizabeth Grosz's (2011) critique of intersectionality theory. Intersectionality considers structures and categories such as patriarchy, gender, race and religion as well as concepts such as 'man' and 'woman' and analyses how these concepts and structures interact, intersect and overlap so as to understand complex socio-economic problems such as inequality, injustice and other forms of oppression (p. 6). Yet as Grosz (2007) argues, this model presumes these single structures and categories exist, whereas in fact they are reified abstractions, and cannot account for the complexity of unpredictable and dynamic events.

By dismantling the autonomous, independent subject, and cultivating an intellectual environment where everything is in a state of flux and change, post structural theory troubles inclusion, by questioning both the constructed subject and the socio-political context that minorities want to be a part of. As Grosz (2011) explains, intersectionality theory bases the notion of inclusion on outdated social structures, such as patriarchy, remaining tethered to the very same forces of oppression and 'multiplying more of the same', thus failing to consider alternative socio-political environment to come (p. 84). The alternative proposed by Grosz, is to conceive of identity differently, not in relation or subordination to another, but rather to generate models of inclusion based on a celebration of diversity and difference, which is a generative force that challenges mainstream notions of identity and thus generates new socio-political environments (pp. 89–91).

For PhD students and supervisors, this complex task requires a robust understanding of the factors that contribute to the construction of a scholarly identity, as well as the dismantling of habitual modes of thinking and perceiving, so as to conceptualise the social, political and intellectual milieu in which PhD research occurs. Thinking with theory can thus be used to provide rich intellectual environments that broaden the notion of inclusive education and research practices, which means including students within a broader intellectual context. For Martin and Kamberelis (2013), research of this kind is 'critical and has political teeth' (p. 673), which for Whitburn (2016) 'grind(s) through the core issues that motivate exclusion' (p. 120).

8   The Queen Street Project

Responding to the contextualised problems identified in this chapter, the Queen Street Project set out to create an environment of belonging to the academy by including PhD students in a supportive, collaborative and challenging academic environment. Regular seminars and the establishment of community for isolated PhD students is not a new idea, but is less frequently seen. As supervisors respond to increasing levels of pressure to accommodate requirements for university-led teaching approaches, quantified research outputs and service, their time is limited which has consequences for PhD students (White, 2012).

The purpose of this project was to assist PhD candidates to complete their theses with access to theories and familiarity with them leading to ways of thinking that went beyond their own reading and the knowledge of their overburdened supervisors. It also aimed to better inform students about working in universities after the PhD has been completed. Gaining employment or postdoctoral positions tends to be predicated upon a list of publications being developed alongside the completed PhD thesis. In some Malaysian universities, for example, the PhD will not be awarded until the requisite journal articles are published (White, 2015). Therefore, the Queen Street Project aimed to build community, provide practical assistance with conceptualising and developing theses, ensure relevant and stimulating seminars, support the development of conference presentations, assist with the development of book chapters and journal articles. The overarching purpose of the Queen Street Project was to *include* PhD students in scholarly life, beyond regular supervision meetings, completion of progress reports and the meeting of arbitrarily devised milestones.

A substantial proportion of the participants were concerned about the development of their methodology thesis sections, and a pattern soon became apparent that they had little knowledge of or exposure to theory. The compulsory units of study that the university conducted emphasised compliance with ethics requirements, method (in the sense of technique or procedure) and project design, but a sizable gap was discerned regarding exposure to theory and the ways in which theory could be used within theses. The Queen Street Project team (authors of this chapter) developed an outline of a proposed program about theory and sought funding for a structured course. The focus was on the complex theoretical milieu of the 'posts', so that PhD students could access and contribute to broader contemporary intellectual discussions operating at the international level. Assisting these students to locate their theses within the current intellectual climate and contribute to this knowledge was a key aim of the Queen St Project. In addition to supporting PhD students to hone their intellectual skills, encouraging them to 'think with theory' was also seen as important. By aiming to create a supportive environment in which students could experiment with theories, talk about their work with other students from various disciplines and gain confidence in doing so, may also assist in the development of individual scholarly identity. By developing confidence that they could also belong to international intellectual communities, students began to consider how they could attend conferences and contribute to publications with scholars who were grappling with similar issues.

The Queen Street Project was conducted over ten weeks in five afternoon sessions, called the 'Theory Circles'. The course was developed to expose students from diverse faculties within one university to current trends in post structural theories and post qualitative research. The course was loosely based on the 'Writing Circles'/'Writing Groups' model (de Ryker, 2014; Aitchison, 2014), where students would regularly meet to write to share and discuss their work. In Theory Circles students read articles related to the themes of power, difference, subjectivity and inclusion. The pedagogical model was structured around reading, discussing, listening, presenting and writing, so that students had the opportunity to work with the material in detail. A supportive environment was cultivated where students could consider and experiment with new ways of thinking and doing research without noticing the pressure of timely completion requirements.

A useful metaphor for the process observed in Theory Circles is the development of intellectual GPS processes related to individual research interests. This meant the students began to locate themselves within broader academic intellectual frameworks, that enhanced their sense of belonging and confidence for bolder conceptualisation, theorisation and writing of their research projects. Students examined recent trends in post structural, post qualitative and post human areas such as crip theory (McRuer, 2006), post colonialism (Bignall, 2014) and auto ethnography (de Freitas & Paton, 2009), as well as feminism and agency (Grosz, 2010) and critical readings about interviews and voice (Mazzei, 2016). Whitburn (2016) offers a useful illustration of this in his discussion about the structure of interview questions that deconstruct the binary between interviewer and interviewee by asking open-ended questions of young people at risk of being marginalised in schools that allows 'unanticipated stories and statements' to emerge (Charmaz, 2014, p. 65).

While the formal evaluation of the course indicates that the Theory Circles part of the Queen Street Project, was successful and raised important issues for PhD students, it was a pilot project that always had a precarious future. The course was offered again in 2017 and a new Part 2 course was added that focused on using theory to think with research data and put theory to work in specific research projects. Employment of theory in research is important but it is also a very time consuming part of the PhD project. The Theory Circles program also attracted interest from some PhD supervisors which led to the idea of a Theory Circles course for supervisors. Given the significant and competing demands on their time, the contemporary academic in the modernized university is sorely pressed, so a structured overview course like the one we developed is useful. Like much within the managed university, however, these proposals will all depend upon funding and priorities. Theory doesn't feature explicitly in mandated university courses for PhD students. Nor are supervisors required to comment on the development of theoretical knowledge in formal progress reports on PhD students. It is only when international examiners weigh and appraise a thesis for its unique contribution to knowledge, that the significance of theory comes to the fore.

9 Conclusion

In this chapter, how PhD candidates may be supported to belong within the academy has been considered. By troubling the notion of inclusion via post structural theory, and experimenting with the inclusive model of belonging at the heart of the Queen Street Project, we have sought to address tensions between the complexity of developing a PhD that generates an original contribution to knowledge with the constraints of the managed academic environment. By considering post structural theories and the ontological turn, we have attempted to demonstrate how learning to think with theory challenges assumptions behind the isolated, independent subject. In this way, PhD scholarship has been contextualized within environments of change, a learning through belonging to a community and as part of the process of becoming. A rich and stimulating intellectual milieu will always serve to trouble habituated research practices. We sought to create such an environment in the Queen Street Project where students undertook complex learning tasks to think more creatively and openly with theory and to confidently begin to apply theory within their own research projects. Thinking with post structural theories can be a daunting task if done alone but our project suggests a way forward for universities to appreciate and value different knowledges, different ontologies and different research methodologies, beyond what is already known.

References

Aitchison, C. (2014). Learning from multiple voices: Feedback and authority in doctoral writing groups. In C. Aitchison & C. Guerin (Eds.), *Writing groups for doctoral education and beyond: Innovations in practice and theory* (pp. 51–64). London: Routledge.

Atkinson, P., Delamont, S., & Parry, O. (2000). *The doctoral experience: Success and failure in graduate school*. London: Falmer Press.

Barad, K. (2007). *Meeting the universe halfway: Quantum physics and the entanglement of matter and meaning*. Durham, NC: Duke University Press.

Beck, J., & Young, M. F. (2005). The assault on the professions and the restructuring of academic and professional identities: A Bernsteinian analysis. *British Journal of Sociology of Education, 26*(2), 183–197.

Bignall, S. (2014). The collaborative struggle for excolonialism. *Settler Colonial Studies, 4*(4), 340–356. doi:10.1080/2201473x.2014.911651

Braidotti, R. (2010). Of poststructuralist ethics and nomadic subjects. In M. Duwell, C. Rehmann-Sutter, & D. Mieth (Eds.), *The contingent nature of life: Bioethics and limits of human existence* (pp. 25–36). Dordrecht: Springer.

Charmaz, K. (2014). *Constructing grounded theory* (2nd ed.). London: Sage Publications.

Cribb, A., & Gewirtz, S. (2006). Doctoral student supervision in a managerial climate. *International Studies in Sociology of Education, 16*(3), 223–236.

de Freitas, E., & Paton, J. (2009). (De) facing the self: Poststructural disruptions of the autoethnographic text. *Qualitative Inquiry, 15*(3), 483–498.

Deleuze, G. (1995). Letter to a harsh critic (M. Joughin, Trans.). In G. Deleuze (Ed.), *Negotiations: 1972–1990* (pp. 3–12). New York, NY: Columbia University Press.

Deleuze, G. (1997). Literature and life. *Critical Inquiry, 23*(2), 225–230.

De Rycker, A. (2014) How do postgraduate students recontextualise "doing research" as a social practice? A critical analysis using Van Leeuwen's socio-semantic model. *Journal of Academic Language and Learning, 8*(1), A48–A61. Retrieved from http://journal.aall.org.au/index.php/jall/article/view/310

Devos, A. (2005). *Mentoring, women and the construction of academic identities* (Unpublished doctoral thesis). University of Technology, Sydney.

Devos, A., & Somerville, M. (2012). What constitutes doctoral knowledge? Exploring issues of power and subjectivity in doctoral examination. *Australian Universities' Review, 54*(1), 47–54.

Foucault, M. (1982). The subject and power. *Critical Inquiry, 8*(4), 777–795.

Grosz, E. (2007). *Keynote address.* Paper presented at the Feminist Theory Workshop, Duke University, Durham, NC. Retrieved February 3, 2012, from http://www.youtube.com/watch?v=mwHoswjw5yo

Grosz, E. (2010). The untimeliness of feminist theory. *NORA: Nordic Journal of Feminist and Gender Research, 18*(1), 48–51.

Grosz, E. (2011). *Becoming undone: Darwinian reflections on life, politics, and art.* Durham, NC: Duke University Press.

Guttorm, H. E., Hohti, R., & Paakkari, A. (2015). "Do the next thing": An interview with Elizabeth Adams St. Pierre on post-qualitative methodology. *Reconceptualizing Educational Research Methodology, 6*(1), 15–22.

Harwood, V., Hickey-Moody, A., McMahon, S., & O'Shea, S. (2016). *The politics of widening participation and university access for young people: Making educational futures.* London: Routledge.

Jackson, A. Y. (2013). Posthumanist data analysis of mangling practices. *International Journal of Qualitative Studies in Education, 26*(6), 741–748. doi:10.1080/09518398.2013.788762

Jackson, A. Y., & Mazzei, L. A. (2012). *Thinking with theory in qualitative research: Viewing data across multiple perspectives.* New York, NY: Routledge.

Kamler, B., & Thomson, P. (2006). *Helping doctoral students write: Pedagogies for supervision.* London: Routledge.

Lather, P., & St. Pierre, E. A. (2013). Post-qualitative research. *International Journal of Qualitative Studies in Education, 26*(6), 629–633. doi:10.1080/09518398.2013.788752

Law, J. (2004). *After method: Mess in social science research.* London: Routledge.

MacLure, M. (2010). The offence of theory. *Journal of Education Policy, 25*(2), 277–286.

Martin, A. D., & Kamberelis, G. (2013). Mapping not tracing: Qualitative educational research with political teeth. *International Journal of Qualitative Studies in Education, 26*(6), 668–679.

Mazzei, L. A. (2016). Voice without a subject. *Cultural Studies↔ Critical Methodologies*, *16*(2), 151–161.

McCoy, K. (2012). Toward a methodology of encounters: Opening to complexity in qualitative research. *Qualitative Inquiry*, *18*(9), 762–772. doi:10.1177/1077800412453018

McRuer, R. (2006). *Crip theory: Cultural signs of queerness and disability*. New York, NY: NYU Press.

Miller, L., Whalley, J. B., & Stronach, I. (2005). From structuralism to poststructuralism. In B. Somekh & C. Lewin (Eds.), *Research methods in the social sciences* (pp. 310–317). Thousand Oaks, CA: Sage Publications.

O'Farrell, C. (2005). *Michel Foucault*. Thousand Oaks, CA: Sage Publications.

Petersen, E. B. (2007). Negotiating academicity: Postgraduate research supervision as category boundary work. *Studies in Higher Education*, *32*(4), 475–487. doi:10.1080/03075070701476167

Rizvi, F. (2008). Speaking truth to power: Edward said and the work of the intellectual. In J. Satterthwaite, M. Watts, & H. Piper (Eds.), *Talking truth, confronting power* (pp. 113–126). Stoke on Trent: Trentham Books.

Rose, G. (1997). Situating knowledges: Positionality, reflexivities and other tactics. *Progress in Human Geography*, *21*(3), 305–320.

Shildrick, M. (2012). Critical disability studies: Rethinking the conventions for the age of postmodernity. In N. Watson, A. Roulstone, & C. Thomas (Eds.), *Routledge handbook of disability studies* (pp. 30–41). London: Routledge.

Shore, C. (2010). Beyond the multiversity: Neoliberalism and the rise of the schizophrenic university. *Social Anthropology*, *18*(1), 15–29.

Slee, R. (2011). *The irregular school: Exclusion, schooling and inclusive education*. London: Routledge.

St. Pierre, E. A. (2004). Deleuzian concepts for education: The subject undone. *Educational Philosophy and Theory*, *36*(3), 283–296. doi:10.1111/j.1469-5812.2004.00068.x

St. Pierre, E. A. (2009). Afterword: Decentering voice in qualitative inquiry. In A. Y. Jackson & L. A. Mazzei (Eds.), *Voice in qualitative inquiry: Challenging conventional, interpretive, and critical conceptions in qualitative research*. London & New York: Routledge.

St. Pierre, E. A. (2011a). Post qualitative research: The critique and the coming after. In N. K. Denzin & Y. S. Lincoln (Eds.), *The Sage handbook of qualitative research* (4th ed., pp. 611–626). Thousand Oaks, CA: Sage Publications.

St. Pierre, E. A. (2011b). Refusing human being in humanist qualitative research. In N. K. Denzin & M. D. Giardina (Eds.), *Qualitative inquiry and global crises* (pp. 40–55). Walnut Creek, CA: Left Coast Press.

St. Pierre, E. A. (2013). The posts continue: Becoming. *International Journal of Qualitative Studies in Education*, *26*(6), 646–657. doi:10.1080/09518398.2013.788754

Utley, A. (2001, July). Outbreak of 'new managerialism' infects faculties. *Times Higher Education Supplement.* Retrieved August 15, 2013, from https://www.timeshighereducation.com/news/outbreak-of-new-managerialism-infects-faculties/164003

Whitburn, B. (2016). Voice, post-structural representation and the subjectivity of 'included' students. *International Journal of Research & Method in Education, 39*(2), 117–130. doi:10.1080/1743727X.2014.946497

White, J. (2012). Scholarly identity. In T. Fitzgerald, H. Gunter, & J. White (Eds.), *Hard labour? Academic work and the changing landscape of higher education* (pp. 42–67). Bingley: Emerald.

White, J. (2013). Doctoral education and new managerialism. In M. Vicars & T. McKenna (Eds.), *Discourse, power, and resistance down under* (pp. 187–194). Rotterdam, The Netherlands: Sense Publishers.

White, J. (2015). Shaping PhD researchers: Fearless intellectuals or managed employees? *Malaysian Journal of Qualitative Research, 11*(1), 1–17.

CHAPTER 5

Achieving Citizenship for All
Theorising Active Participation for Disabled Children and Their Families in Early Childhood Education

Kate McAnelly and Michael Gaffney

1   Introduction

Aotearoa New Zealand's education headlines are frequently dominated by stories of disabled children, including those in early childhood education (ECE), being excluded, marginalised and disempowered. The social, cultural and political barriers that these children and their families encounter just enrolling in and attending ECE settings, let alone fully engaging in learning, can be immense. In this article, we contend that all members of early childhood communities of practice have a crucial role to play, and carry a mantle of responsibility, in supporting the active participation of disabled children and their families in the everyday programme. In order to do this we require a theoretical framework to expand our understanding of participation and inclusion. We draw on current theory to refine our current aspirations for all our tamariki in terms of inclusive teaching and learning environments, where everyone is able to realise and practice citizenship as a matter of fundamental human rights.

2   The Backstory

Kate's son, Stephen, began attending a preschool close to their home just prior to his 2nd birthday in August 2008. Kate and her husband Dave were somewhat unsure if Stephen would even be accepted onto their roll as he was what their Plunket[1] nurse had described as "developmentally curious". He had developed according to typical expected milestones until the age of 15 months, at which point he lost all of his previously acquired language and retreated into a world of his own making. Kate and Dave, first time parents, wondered if it was just a stage children went through, and they were still waiting for the Stephen of old to emerge when they received a call to inform them that a spot had come up for Stephen at the preschool. He had been on the waiting list for some time. Nervously they explained Stephen's difference to the preschool manager, who swept aside their concerns and said Stephen would be most welcome at the centre.

However the welcome mat that had been so quickly rolled out for Stephen and his family was just as quickly rolled away. Barriers, especially of the attitudinal variety, to their active participation in the preschool programme became readily apparent. The preschool also aggressively insisted that Stephen's unnamed difference, which they were initially so willing to work with, be quantified as they felt they could not support Stephen's continued attendance at the preschool without the Special Education[2] resourcing an official diagnosis would enable. These events coincided with the birth of Kate and Dave's third child and thus ensued Kate's rapid descent into a vicious cycle of depression and grief. Eventually this emotional labour came to an end and Kate slowly learned to accept and embrace Stephen's difference rather than reject and work against it.

By the time Stephen received an official diagnosis of autism spectrum disorder in November 2009, three months after his third birthday, her eyes were beginning to open to the fact that Stephen was not being included by virtue of his physical presence at the preschool, as she had previously thought. The exclusionary culture within the centre was such that Stephen's early intervention teacher politely suggested that Kate and Dave find somewhere else more accepting of diverse learners for Stephen to attend. Yet Kate refused, because as she recalls, "where else would I find a place where Stephen was allowed to attend?". She was so mired in the charity and pity disability discourses (Shakespeare, 2014) that were so visible in what members of the preschool community said and did that she had come to genuinely believe that the preschool was doing her a favour in allowing poor autistic Stephen to be there. So Stephen stayed, as did his experience of discrimination.

By the time Stephen's last three months at the preschool arrived prior to him starting school, the bubbling discrimination had become a festering sore. Kate had finally realised that Stephen was not respected or valued by almost all of the preschool community. A teacher who had been there for a short time that was committed to helping Stephen overcome the barriers to learning and participation that he constantly came up against left the preschool, fed up with stubborn attitudes and policies that were not responsive to diversity. After this, Stephen's preschool experiences really went downhill. He was left to aimlessly wander around each day, and no-one sought to engage him in the programme. When questioned about this, the preschool manager said "don't worry, we just want Stephen to enjoy what's left of his time with us". Kate interpreted this as an indication they were giving up on Stephen, which is precisely what happened. Teachers, children and families began openly speaking of Stephen in terms like 'retard', 'thick', 'idiot', 'freak' and 'stupid'. A revolving series of teachers began to "deal with" Stephen and his needs, rather than the one consistent support person he had been used to. This caused huge anxiety which spilled over into home life. Stephen's toilet training programme that had been so carefully planned out and adhered to was abandoned.

It was also decided that Stephen's attendance at the preschool was contingent on the presence of his Special Education education support worker (ESW). If she could not be there for whatever reason, then neither could Stephen. Even if the ESW was scheduled to be there for only an hour of the full day Stephen was enrolled, if she was absent, then Stephen had to stay away the entire day. In the end, Stephen was present but that was all. He was not participating, engaged or achieving. He had no sense of belonging or that he mattered to his preschool community. He was not vested with knowledge of himself as a competent, confident learner and communicator. His difference was neither honoured, nor was there a commitment to work with it in meaningful ways. His physical wellbeing might have been assured, but his emotional, spiritual and family wellbeing were completely disregarded. Stephen was failed.

These experiences were difficult for Kate to make sense of as a parent. She knew things could, and should, be better in ECE, but what could she personally do about it? It was too late to effect any change for Stephen's situation as he had moved onto school – a beautifully inclusive one at that, for which her heart was extremely glad. She eventually saw a space for herself to become the sort of teacher that Stephen, and disabled children like him, needed and so often do not get. Kate felt that she would be able to draw from her personal experiences and understandings as a parent to inform her professional practice as an educator. She went to teacher's college and after graduating with her early childhood teaching degree combined work as a teacher with further study towards her Postgraduate Diploma in Teaching and then her Master of Education.

3 Meanwhile What of the Current Political Context?

Section 8 of New Zealand's Education Act (1989) refers to "people who have special educational needs (whether because of disability or otherwise) have the same rights to enrol and receive education in state schools as people who do not". There is no mention of the rights of children (whether disabled or not) to enrol at and attend early childhood services, as ECE is not part of the compulsory education sector. This makes ECE contestable and open to various interpretations of what constitutes participation for disabled children.

The vision of the New Zealand Disability Strategy (NZDS) (Office for Disability Issues, 2016) is of a society that highly values and continually enhances the full participation of disabled people in the lives of their local communities. While the previous iteration of the Strategy (Office for Disability Issues, 2001) sought to have the 'best' education possible provided to disabled people, it did not elaborate on what that could or should look like. Furthermore, early childhood education was, although hinted at, not explicitly referred to once in the document. This made ECE contestable and open to interpretation, and rendered disabled children and their families within it invisible. However, the updated Strategy gives specific guidance as to what a quality inclusive education for disabled learners looks like, and ECE is now part of the conversation alongside primary, secondary, tertiary settings.

The United Nations Convention on the Rights of Persons with Disabilities (UNCRPD), which New Zealand ratified in 2008, acknowledges the right of people with disabilities to education, without discrimination, on the basis of equal opportunity with the purpose of achieving "the full development of human potential and sense of dignity and self-worth, and the strengthening of respect for human rights, fundamental freedoms and human diversity" (United Nations, 2006, Article 24). The National government's assertion that New Zealand has a highly inclusive education system where all disabled children can learn, grow and participate alongside their peers in everyday, non-segregated settings is a highly contentious one. New Zealand based research (Macartney, 2009; Purdue, 2004; Purdue, Gordon-Burns, Rarere-Briggs, Stark, & Turnock, 2011) as well as a multitude of narratives from disabled learners and their families (https://autismandoughtisms.wordpress.com; www.bat-bean-beam.blogspot.co.nz; http://publicaddress.net/access/) suggest there are frequently insurmountable barriers to being, knowing and doing experienced at all levels that negatively impact on the ability of disabled learners to realise their right to a quality inclusive education. This is despite having a diversity-friendly curricula in place that should theoretically be able to counter these if the will and commitment to do so by the people enacting them is there.

An earlier government's vision for early childhood education in Aotearoa New Zealand, as outlined in Pathways to the Future: Ngā Huarahi Arataki, A 10-Year Strategic Plan for Early Childhood Education (2002). The aim was to improve the quality of ECE services, promote collaborative relationships and increase participation in ECE, no matter what a child's background or circumstances. Whether this vision has been achieved or not, particularly with regard to the debate on 'quality' ECE, is both debatable and contentious. A new 10 year strategic plan to develop and strengthen early learning in New Zealand was announced in April 2018, and a key objective of this is equitable access to active participation and quality learning for all children, regardless of background or ability. The roll out of this new strategic plan in 2019 offers a lot of hope in guiding inclusive early childhood education towards a new dawn in New Zealand.

Aotearoa New Zealand's early childhood curriculum document Te Whāriki (Ministry of Education, 2017) offers inclusive approaches to the active participation of disabled children and their families in everyday early childhood settings, based on ethical, bicultural and relational understandings of teaching and learning. The original iteration of Te Whāriki (Ministry of Education, 1996) was written with the express intention of challenging and refuting a 'one size fits all' approach to children under 5 and their development (Carr & May, 1993). However, it did not explicitly address the role that early childhood education played in reproducing inequity and exclusion regarding disability. This is especially so where disabled children are explicitly identified and referred to in the document as "children who have special needs (Ministry of Education, 1996, p. 11)". This separatist language or 'specialese' serves to marginalise and exclude disabled children and their families, despite the inclusive intent of the document (Macartney, 2014). The revised Te Whāriki, released in April 2017, has sought to both critically examine the role ECE settings play in reproducing inequity and exclusion of many types, not just regarding disability, and further, has also replaced the term 'special needs' with a more inclusive "diversity of ability and learning needs" (Ministry of Education, 2017, p. 13). These revisions were guided by an increasing conceptualisation of disabled children as competent, able social actors and citizens of their worlds.

The Ministry of Education's Success for All policy (2010) actively promotes the inclusion of all children in school settings. Its Statement of Intent recognises that children with 'special' education needs (described as those who need extra support because of "a physical disability, a sensory impairment, a learning or communication delay, a social, emotional or behavioural difficulty, or a combination of these") have difficulty actively participating in everyday education settings without appropriate supports in place. It also expresses a desire to increase participation rates for disabled children while maintaining high quality education provision for all. ECE is not part of the discussion, yet the ideas of presence, participation, achievement, engagement and belonging emerging from it are equally as relevant and important to disabled learners in ECE settings, who grow up to be disabled learners in primary and secondary settings. The Ministry's operationalisation of participation as disabled learners enrolling at and attending everyday services is of particular concern when the literature suggests active participation points more to equitable, inclusive education for all, not just some (Gabel & Danforth, 2008; Slee, 2011).

4 In Search of a Theoretical Framework?

We were drawn to the participation model Huakina Mai offered by Glynne Mackey and Colleen Lockie (2012) because it was designed as a framework through which to critically examine issues of economic disadvantage and how these impacted on affected children and their families being able to actively participate and practice citizenship within ECE settings. The parallels with disabled children not being able to engage as full citizens in ECE settings was striking. It provides a critique of the current governments focus on participation as enrolment and instead suggests

> Participation does not equate with active participation...Kaiako who understand these distinctions are likely to engage in participation for citizenship discourses that acknowledge that children have agency. This knowledge allows teachers to understand children as competent to make a contribution as active members of society. (p. 84)

This approach provided a valid lens through which to critically examine disability in the same context. There are four levels of participation in ECE settings according to the Huakina Mai model. The first level is enrolment – where children are enrolled at an early childhood service. The second level is attendance – children regularly attend an early childhood service. The third level is ecological participation, where "children and their families engage in a range of experiences offered by the early childhood education setting" (p. 85). Finally, the fourth level is active participation, which is defined as ecological, pedagogic, equitable and inclusive in nature. Accordingly, tamariki and their whānau actively engage in decision making related to daily matters, curriculum/programme, and management and goverance. They are thus able to make a difference to the experiences that are offered with the early childhood education setting, and they practise citizenship (p. 85).

Yet one of its authors, Glynne Mackey, advised that the model had had little real-life application that she was aware of, and recommended that we look to the works of British early childhood education researcher Peter Moss, whose work she and the late Colleen Lockie had drawn on when drawing up the model, to 'flesh out' our understandings of what active participation might look like in practice (personal communication).

Ecological participation, Moss (2007) suggests, relies very much on how members of communities of practice are conceptualised. This speaks strongly to how inclusive practice is enacted within 'children's spaces' that are valued as sites for many possibilities and projects, be they social, cultural, economic, political, ethical, aesthetic or whatever else (Moss & Petrie, 2002). Accordingly, the image of the child is of an active subject, a multi-lingual creator of knowledge and identity from birth, connected in relations of interdependency with other children and adults, a citizen with rights, rich in potential, a human being not human becoming, competent, intelligent and imbued with rights and strengths (Malaguzzi, 1994). The image of the teacher is of an engaged, competent learner, a researcher and critical thinker, a dialogic educator and politically aware child advocate, a challenger and refuter of deficit discourses about disability and difference, with practice based on respectful democratic relationships with stakeholders within and external to their community of practice (Wenger, 1998). Parents and families are positioned as competent citizens who have and develop their own experiences, points of view and ideas. This is coupled with the expectation and responsibility of nurturing the same in their children so all children and their families can actively participate in socially just, equitable, inclusive teaching and learning environments where the realisation and practice of citizenship for all is a promise. An illuminating contextual picture of such a children's space was painted by Associació de Mestres Rosa Sensat (2005, p. 10 in Moss, 2007) who said

> The (kindergarten) must be a place for everyone, a meeting place in the physical but also social, cultural and political sense of the word...where (children and adults) can dialogue, listen and discuss in order to share meanings: it is a place of infinite possibilities...a place of ethical and political praxis, a space for democratic learning. (p. 4)

Pedagogic participation or the how inclusion is enacted in early childhood communities of practice, Moss (2007) asserts, begins with democratic decision making about the purposes, the practices and the environment of the early childhood setting, therefore addressing John Dewey's principle that all participants within education settings must contribute to producing and managing them (Dewey, 1916). Holistic understandings of learning are crucially important, as democratic practice is primarily concerned with going beyond seeing learning solely as reproducing pre-determined content and skills, instead viewing children as primary constructors of their own learning and producers of original points of view concerning the world (Dahlberg & Moss, 2005). Moss draws on pedagogies of freedom (Freire) and listening (Rinaldi) that are open to unpredicted outcomes and new thought, which are thoughtfully integrated in everyday programmes. Curiosity, uncertainty and subjectivity are accordingly welcomed, but alongside the responsibility these demand. He also points to the significance of contesting dominant discourses, what Foucault

(2007) calls 'regimes of truth', in the context of pedagogic participation. These regimes of truth are backed by privileged groups – the government and Ministry of Education especially – who claim a privileged position of 'expertise'. Contesting these powerful discourses, particularly politics of representation in deciding whose perspectives have legitimacy, means striving to make core assumptions and values visible in early childhood settings and welcoming and affirming diversity. This therefore opens up democratic dialogue about what communities of practice consider the 'good life' to be for their learners, and how they wish to attain it.

Moss (2007) and Fielding and Moss (2010) very much advocate for early childhood settings to operate as spaces for participatory democratic practice – the rule of all by all. Such a space, they contend, offers opportunities for all its citizens to actively participate in the things that matter to them. This idea of participation defines early childhood settings as social and political places and thus as educational spaces in the fullest sense. However, Moss warns that this is not a given – it is not a natural, intrinsic part of simply being a community of practice. It is a philosophical choice, a choice a community of practice makes based on values. These communities have respect for and honour diversity, and have an intrinsic understanding of the relational ethics that treats the alterity of the 'other' with respect. They also recognise multiple perspectives and diverse paradigms in their understanding that there is more than one answer to most questions, and that there are many ways of viewing and understanding the world around us. Moss argues that all people are equal and should be respected and valued in democratic early childhood education settings as a matter of basic human rights, a fundamental tenet of inclusive education. This means supporting all children to participate in the cultures, curricula and communities of their local ECE settings. He states that the barriers to learning and participation that children encounter need to be actively reduced using democratic participatory methods so that they feel a sense of belonging and community in the communities of practice of which they are members. Furthermore, he suggests the need for agitation for radical change on the political or macro level, giving extra assurance that ECE services have the resources, understandings, values and commitment to teach all children well in democratic non-discriminatory settings. Moss (2007) summed the significance of equitable, inclusive practice up well when he ventured that

> Democratic participation is an important criterion of citizenship: it is a means by which children and adults can participate with others in shaping decisions affecting themselves (and) groups of which they are members in wider society...it is...a means of resisting power and its will

TABLE 5.1 Defining the concept of active participation

Pedagogic participation	Ecological participation	Inclusive/equitable participation
All members of early childhood communities of practice are actively supported (in whichever ways suit them best)	All members of early childhood communities of practice are conceptualised as having competence, agency and the capacity to learn	All members of early childhood communities of practice are respected and honoured for the diverse understandings and abilities they bring with them
With the aim that all members meaningfully engage in democratic decision-making processes about the things that affect them in their settings.		

to govern, and the forms of oppression and injustice that arise from the unrestrained exercise of power. Last, but not least, [active participation] creates the possibility for diversity to flourish, …[offering] the production of new thinking and new practice (p. 4).

Using the concepts we now have a framework with which to explore children's experiences of participation in education (see Table 5.1).

5   The Search for Active Participation

A number of researchers have positioned disabled learners as having the right to participate in and receive a high quality inclusive early childhood education (Recchia & Lee, 2012; Macartney, 2011; Macartney & Morton, 2009; Purdue, Gordon-Burns, Rarere-Briggs, Stark, & Turnock, 2011). They agree that participation can and does look different from setting to setting, and describe the process by which a setting constructs participation that then allows disabled children and their families to encounter many of the barriers they face in realising that mandated promise of a high quality inclusive education (Purdue et al., 2011). These same authors and others argue that interpretations of what 'participation' looks like for disabled children – be it physical presence, fitting in with normative assumptions about learning and development, or being irrelevant or unimportant to that of their peers and often accepted as inclusive – can and should be challenged and refuted, because they do not view disabled children as being competent or having agency (Recchia & Lee, 2012; Macartney, 2011; Macartney & Morton, 2009; Ministry of Education, 1996; Office for Disability Issues, 2001; Purdue et al., 2011; United Nations, 2006; United Nations, 1990). Instead, these pervasive beliefs serve to limit the active participation of disabled children in everyday ECE settings, and thus deny them the opportunity to realise and practice citizenship. Active participation, they argue, is where disabled children and their families are meaningfully engaged in democratic decision making processes about the things that affect them in everyday ECE settings, thus facilitating an equitable, inclusive teaching and learning environment for all (Recchia & Lee, 2012; Macartney, 2011; Purdue et al., 2011). The New Zealand based authors (Macartney, 2011; Macartney & Morton, 2009; Purdue et al., 2011) in particular query why, with such an array of supportive national legislation and policies (Ministry of Education, 1996; Office for Disability Issues, 2001; United Nations, 2007; United Nations, 1990) that supposedly protects the rights of all children and their families to actively participate in non-discriminatory inclusive early childhood education, it is so difficult to realise those rights in Aotearoa.

5.1   *What Context Did They Work Within?*

The authors all conducted their studies specifically in ECE settings, although they all framed their studies differently. Recchia and Lee (2012) focused on teacher competencies in inclusive early childhood spaces, a key focus being to understand how children begin to learn who (and what) is valued in the social world, why this might be, and to contextualise children's earliest understandings of their own place within, and importance to, the larger community of learners to which they belong. Macartney and Morton (2009) critiqued how dominant deficit discourses influence teachers and special education 'experts' to accept the participation of disabled children in everyday ECE settings at the 'enrolment' and 'attendance' levels outlined in the Huakina Mai model (Mackey & Lockie, 2012) described above. Macartney (2011) discussed what an inclusive community of learners in an early childhood setting looks like, with particular attention on the responsibility of the community of learners to promote diversity and difference as positive attributes, and ensure the full and meaningful participation of children with disabilities and their families. This was compared with the effect of 'normalising judgements' (barriers) on disabled children and their families being able to actively participate in, and have full membership of, everyday ECE settings. Purdue et al. (2011) engaged with a wide variety of everyday ECE stakeholders (disabled children, their families, teachers and the wider community of practice) to see how these communities and the members within them included disabled children and their families. They then discussed how the active participation of disabled children and their families can still elicit significant negativity from other children and their families, teachers, centre managers and specialist education support professionals, who struggle to understand their legally mandated, moral and ethical obligations to support such participation as a matter of right (Kliewer, Biklen, & Kasa-Hendrickson, 2006; Stark, Gordon-Burns, Purdue, Rarere-Briggs, & Turnock, 2011).

5.2 Disability Studies in Education

Three of the four studies (Recchia & Lee, 2012; Macartney, 2011; Macartney & Morton, 2009) used concepts from Disability Studies in Education (DSE) (Baglieri, Valle, Connor, & Gallagher, 2010). DSE promotes the understanding of disability as being socially and politically constructed, and seeks to challenge and eliminate the barriers to being and doing that learners with disabilities may encounter as they progress through education (Connor, Gabel, Gallagher, & Morton, 2008). A central line of questioning in DSE scholarship is to ask what inclusive education is, who is included, and why. The interests, voices and privilege of disabled students in their education are foregrounded. DSE rejects deficit models of disability and assumes that all children have the right to equitable, full, and meaningful access to a quality, inclusive education (Gabel, 2005; Valle & Connor, 2011). Purdue et al. (2011) used an interpretivist approach, which was about seeking to understand children with disabilities and their families in a world where their lived realities are socially mediated, open to change and complex. The main thrust for interpretivist researchers is to strive to learn about a particular issue from people who are experiencing the issues being researched (O'Donoghue, 2006). Additionally, Macartney (2011) referred to Foucauldian discourse analysis, which examines power relationships in society as expressed through language and practices (Foucault, 1977; Foucault, 1980). Further to Foucault, Macartney (2011) and Macartney and Morton (2009) also made mention of four specific pedagogies, Paulo Freire's pedagogies of hope, freedom and the oppressed, and Carlina Rinaldi's pedagogy of listening. Freire's pedagogy of hope describes hope as an ontological need that should be anchored in practice in order to become concrete, further stating that without hope, we cannot begin the struggle to effect lasting change (Freire & Freire, 1998). His pedagogy of freedom positions teaching as an ethical and political act, saying that there is no teaching without learning, teaching is not just a simple transfer of knowledge, and describing teaching as deeply humanising and humbling (Freire, 1998). Finally, his pedagogy of the oppressed explores various notions of power, knowledge and mediation between oppressors/colonisers/more learned others and the oppressed/colonised/less learned others (Freire, 1970).

Rinaldi's pedagogy of listening (Rinaldi, 2001) is based on two broad aspects, both involving relationships with/in the social and physical environments of early childhood education (Rinaldi having long been associated with the Reggio Emilia movement). One aspect involves children's and adult's search for meaning and understanding through listening. That is, not just actively hearing/listening, although that is of course important, but also thinking about patterns that connect us together and to others, having the openness and sensitivity to listen and be listened to using all our senses. This listening ties into Malaguzzi's hundred languages of children, as does time, attention and emotions, as well as being open and welcoming of diversity and difference. It is an active verb that legitimises us and gives us visibility as well as the premise for a solid learning relationship. The other aspect encompasses a more political approach, which requires democratic, inclusive dialogue with/in the community of learners and the culture/s in which it operates (Rinaldi, 2006).

5.3 The Link between Participation, Learning, Inclusion and Citizenship

The authors (Recchia & Lee, 2012; Macartney, 2011; Macartney & Morton, 2009; Purdue et al., 2011) all agree that inclusion begins by recognising that all children and their families have the right to access a high quality inclusive early childhood education, and that this right is not affected by disability. They assert that in order to be inclusive, an entire early childhood community of practice (children, teachers, 'specialist' teachers and support staff, parents, families and the wider community to which all of the above might be connected) is responsible for actively identifying and removing barriers to full acceptance, participation and learning for disabled children and their families.

The authors also recognise that many challenges associated with disability are universal and are embedded in sociocultural attitudes and practices. Many of these practices position children under the age of 5 as bothersome or irrelevant, and people with disabilities as other or less than; therefore, the authors contend that children under 5 with disabilities are doubly discriminated against. Thus they are doubly in need of an ongoing commitment on the part of their ECE communities of practice to uphold and honour their right to have full membership of, and actively participate in, those settings. These authors go on to say that inclusive practice on the part of a community of learners does not entail a narrow, rigid, one-size-fits-all 'pigeonholing' of disabled children and their expected achievement, but instead seeks to recognise and respond to their diversity, without isolating and removing them from everyday activities and learning in the setting. Members of an inclusive community of practice think about the child as a learner first. Their disability is secondary to this primary identity. The authors characterise inclusive ECE communities of learners as ones where members did not simply tolerate or accommodate disabled children and their families, but communicated an ethos of fairness, equality and providing a space that is underpinned by principles of active participation, inclusion and citizenship in the promotion of a quality education for all (Ballard, 2013; Booth, Ainscow, & Kingston, 2006).

An important part of the process of building an inclusive early childhood community of practice, the authors state, is to intentionally develop collaborative, responsive, respectful, reciprocal relationships within that community. Everyone has an important role to play in ensuring disabled children and their families feel like they belong and have a place. This includes teachers, specialists, parents, families and the wider community, but also other children attending the setting, who the authors argue play a powerful role in an inclusive setting in challenging, refuting and dismantling sociocultural deficit constructs of difference. All community members are 'on the same page' and support each other to build and maintain an inclusive environment. The authors acknowledge that this process can sometimes be problematic and 'messy', but needs to be respectfully engaged with as the participation, inclusion and citizenship of children with disabilities (and their families) is not contestable, it is a human rights issue (Smith, 2007). Finally, the authors argue that an inclusive community of practice needs to 'push against' the idea that Special Education staff are the 'experts' on disabled children (Runswick-Cole & Hodge, 2009). This is an identity, they assert, to be given first to disabled children themselves, who need to be offered meaningful opportunities to make representations in having a say about the things that concern them. The next best thing to experts on children's lives are their parents and families. Thus, the authors state that parents and families of disabled children, as well as the children themselves, need to be treated as equal and valued members of the 'teaching' team in terms of addressing what and who matters, and why/when, with regard to how their community of practice conceptualises disability and difference.

6 Conclusion – Realising the Practice of Citizenship

It has been a long, hard and often painful road that Kate has navigated translating her personal knowledge as a mum into professional practice as a teacher and researcher. The highly inclusive culture and community her son Stephen and the wider family have enjoyed at school since he started there in 2011 stands in sharp relief to the demoralising neverending battle they faced in Stephen's early childhood years to have him recognised and valued as being one in his humanity with his peers. He was not supported to actively participate in, or have an effect on, the things that mattered to him at his preschool. Instead, he was situated as a 'problem' by that community of practice and from there the deficit thinking and constructions of his dis/ability flowed agonisingly thick and fast for his family. Kate did not feel she could dare to imagine better for Stephen, and that sadness is still with her today. Engaging in research has shown us the possibilities for inclusive early childhood communities of practice when all its members are 'on the same page' with regards to the rights, not needs, of disabled children and their families to actively participate, belong and have a true place in those communities as their Tūrangawaewae.[3] The next step is to make these spaces visible by celebrating them, so that disabled children and their families will be able to begin not just imagining better, but realising it too. It is the very least they deserve.

Notes

1 The name given to a paediatric nurse (employed by a non-government organisation), who is universally available to families in New Zealand.
2 The name given to that part of the Ministry of Education in Aotearoa New Zealand responsible for supporting disabled children. That part of the Ministry is now call Learning Support.
3 The Māori term for a place where one has the right to stand.

References

Baglieri, S., Valle, J., Connor, D., & Gallagher, D.(2010). *Disability studies in education: The need for a plurality of perspectives on disability.* Retrieved from http://www.researchgate.net

Ballard, K. (2013). Thinking in another way: Ideas for sustainable inclusion. *International Journal of Inclusive Education, 17*(8), 762–775.

Booth, T., Ainscow, M., & Kingston, D. (2006). *Index for inclusion: Developing play, learning and participation in early years and childcare.* Retrieved from http://www.researchgate.net

Carr, M., & May, H. (1993). Choosing a model: Reflecting on the development process of Te Whāriki: National early childhood curriculum guidelines in New Zealand. *International Journal of Early Years Education, 1*(3), 7–22.

Connor, D., Gabel, S., Gallagher, D., & Morton, M. (2008). Disability studies and inclusive education: Implications for theory, research, and practice. *International Journal of Inclusive Education, 12*(6), 441–457.

Dahlberg, G., & Moss, P. (2005). *Ethics and politics in early childhood education.* Abingdon: RoutledgeFalmer.

Dewey, J. (1916). *Democracy and education: An introduction to the philosophy of education.* New York, NY: Macmillan.

Fielding, M., & Moss, P. (2010). *Radical education and the common school: A democratic alternative.* Retrieved from http://www.researchgate.net

Foucault, M. (1977). *Discipline and punish: The birth of the prison.* New York, NY: Vintage Books.

Foucault, M. (1980). *Power/knowledge: Selected interviews and other writings.* New York, NY: Pantheon.

Foucault, M. (2007). *Abnormal: Lectures at the collège de France, 1974–1975.* New York, NY: Picador.

Freire, P. (1970). *Pedagogy of the oppressed.* New York, NY: Herder & Herder.

Freire, P. (1998). *Pedagogy of freedom: Ethics, democracy, and civic courage.* Lanham, MD: Rowman & Littlefield.

Freire, P., & Freire, A. (1998). *Pedagogy of the heart.* New York, NY: Continuum.

Gabel, S. (2005). *Disability studies in education: Readings in theory and method.* New York, NY: Peter Lang.

Gabel, S., & Danforth, S. (2008). *Disability and the politics of education: An international reader.* New York, NY: Peter Lang.

Kliewer, C., Biklen, D., & Kasa-Hendrickson, C. (2006). Who may be literate? Disability and resistance to the cultural denial of competence. *American Educational Research Journal, 43*(2), 163–192.

Macartney, B. (2009). Understanding and responding to the tensions between deficit discourses and inclusive education. *SET: Research Information for Teachers, 1,* 19–27.

Macartney, B. (2011). *Disabled by the discourse: Two families' narratives of inclusion, exclusion and resistance in education.* Retrieved from http://www.canterbury.ac.nz

Macartney, B. (2014). How 'specialese' maintains dual education systems in Aotearoa, New Zealand. In R. Wills, M. Morton, M. McLean, M. Stephenson, & R. Slee (Eds.), *Tales from school* (pp. 165–179). Rotterdam, The Netherlands: Sense Publishers.

Macartney, B., & Morton, M. (2011). *Kinds of participation: Teacher and special education perceptions and practices of 'inclusion' in early childhood and primary school settings.* Retrieved from http://www.researchgate.net

Mackey, G., & Lockie, C. (2012). Huakina mai: Opening doorways for children's participation within early childhood settings: Economic disadvantage as a barrier to citizenship. In D. Gordon-Burns, A. Gunn, K. Purdue, & N. Surtees (Eds.), *Te Aotūroa*

Tataki: Inclusive early childhood education: Perspectives on inclusion, social justice and equity in Aotearoa New Zealand (pp. 75–93). Wellington: NZCER Press.

Malaguzzi, L. (1994). *Your image of the child: Where teaching begins*. Retrieved from http://www.reggioalliance.org

Ministry of Education. (1996). *Te Whāriki: He whāriki mātauranga mō ngā mokopuna o Aotearoa: Early childhood curriculum*. Wellington: Learning Media.

Ministry of Education. (2002). *Pathways to the future: Ngā Huarahi Arataki, A ten year strategic plan for early childhood education*. Wellington: Ministry of Education.

Ministry of Education. (2010). *Success for all: Every school, every child*. Retrieved from http://www.education.govt.nz/assets/Documents/School/Inclusive-education/SuccessForAllEnglish.pdf

Morton, M. (2014). *Using DSE to 'notice, recognise and respond' to tools of exclusion and opportunities for inclusion in New Zealand*. Retrieved from http://www.hawaii.edu

Moss, P. (2007). *Bringing politics into the nursery: Early childhood education as a democratic practice*. Retrieved from http://www.researchgate.net

Moss, P., & Petrie, P. (2002). *From children's services to children's spaces: Public policy, children and childhood*. London: RoutledgeFalmer.

New Zealand Government. (1989). *Education act 1989*. Retrieved from http://www.legislation.govt.nz

O'Donoghue, T. (2006). *Planning your qualitative research project: An introduction to interpretivist research in education*. New York, NY: Routledge.

Office for Disability Issues. (2001). *New Zealand disability strategy*. Retrieved from http://www.odi.govt.nz/nzds/

Purdue, K. (2004). *Inclusion and exclusion in early childhood education: Three case studies*. Retrieved from http://www.otago.ac.nz

Purdue, K., Gordon-Burns, D., Rarere-Briggs, B., Stark, R., & Turnock, K. (2011). The exclusion of children with disabilities in early childhood education in New Zealand: Issues and implications for inclusion. *Australasian Journal of Early Childhood, 36*(2), 95–107.

Recchia, S., & Lee, Y. (2012). *Inclusion in the early childhood classroom: What makes a difference?* New York, NY: Teachers College Press.

Rinaldi, C. (2001). The pedagogy of listening: The listening perspective from Reggio Emilia. *Innovations in Early Education: The International Reggio Exchange, 8*(4), 1–4.

Rinaldi, C. (2006). *In dialogue with Reggio Emilia: Listening, researching and learning*. New York, NY: Routledge.

Runswick-Cole, K., & Hodge, N. (2009). Needs or rights? A challenge to the discourse of special education. *British Journal of Special Education, 36*(4), 198–203.

Shakespeare, T. (2014). *Disability rights and wrongs revisited*. New York, NY: Routledge.

Slee, R. (2011). How do we make inclusive education happen when exclusion is a political predisposition? *International Journal of Inclusive Education, 17*(8), 895–907.

Smith, A. (2007). Children and young people's participation rights in education. *The International Journal of Children's Rights, 15*(1), 147–164.

Stark, R., Gordon-Burns, D., Purdue, K., Rarere-Briggs, B., & Turnock, K. (2011). Other parents' perceptions of disability and inclusion in early childhood education: Implications for the teachers' role in creating inclusive communities. *He Kupu, 2*(4), 4–18.

State Services Commission. (2013). *Increase participation in early childhood education.* Retrieved from http://www.ssc.govt.nz/bps-supporting-vulnerable-children

United Nations. (1990). *Convention on the rights of the child.* Retrieved from http://www.ohchr.org/en/professionalinterest/pages/crc.aspx

United Nations. (2006). *Convention on the rights of persons with disabilities.* Retrieved from http://www.un.org/disabilities/convention/

Valle, J., & Connor, D. (2011). *Rethinking disability: A disability studies approach to inclusive practices.* New York, NY: McGraw-Hill.

Wenger, E. (1998). *Communities of practice: Learning, meaning and identity.* Cambridge: Cambridge University Press.

PART 2

Policy and Theory to Support Belonging

CHAPTER 6

The Construction of Giftedness in Education Policy in New Zealand and Australia

Implications for Inclusive Education Policy and Practice

Melanie Wong and Ben Whitburn

1   Introduction

Despite attempts in Australia and New Zealand to make their education systems inclusive of all, equitable provision of educational services to children and young people who fall into particular diagnostic categories remains uneven. Giftedness and twice-exceptionality (2E) is identified in education policy in both countries (Department of Education and Early Childhood Development [DEECD], 2014; New Zealand Ministry of Education, 2012) that explicitly address the educational needs of these learners. These policies emphasise broadened capabilities among gifted and 2E children and the importance of providing them modified programs. However where this does occur, discrepancies persist in program provision (Jarvis & Henderson, 2014, 2015; Long, Barnett, & Rogers, 2015; Plunkett & Kronborg, 2007; Wormald, Vialle, & Rogers, 2014). The purpose of this chapter is to explore how policy in both country contexts construct giftedness and twice-exceptionality in relation to education, and in so doing, legitimate restricted knowledge that limits the participation of children and their families in schooling. We highlight these concerns to consider implications for policy, practice and pedagogy for the inclusion of gifted and 2E children and young people in schools in both countries going forward.

This study is framed using social constructionist theory (Corcoran, 2017) to explore the effects of policy through its social justice intent of inclusive opportunity (Gale & Molla, 2015; Terzi, 2014) for gifted and 2E learners. In its presentation we draw on findings of doctoral research that explores the observations of parents of children with giftedness about their experiences of education. This study revealed that parents' concerns centre on the competitiveness of schools, wherein results are prioritised over learning experiences. We conclude the chapter by highlighting implications of these findings for inclusive education policy contexts.

2. Study Background

Underpinning this chapter is a study conducted by Mel for her PhD, together with further analysis of this material in relation to policy implications for the education of gifted and 2e children and young people. Mel collected qualitative data via a closed Facebook group that facilitated prolonged discussions with parents of children labelled either gifted or twice-exceptional. Discussion topics included defining giftedness, defining equality and equity, reflecting on diversity, provision for gifted children in early childhood settings and primary school settings, and how teachers respond to giftedness. Mel's analysis concluded that parents' concerns centred primarily on the competitiveness of schools and the adverse implications of this on the learning experiences afforded their son or daughter. Furthering the analysis into the study of policy, we seek to focus on how education policy constructs giftedness; specifically how limited notions of learner capability (Gale & Molla, 2015) can lead to these discrepancies. Before presenting this work, we first turn to a presentation of the theoretical framework that underpins the analysis.

3. Framing the Research – Social Constructionism, Giftedness, and Capability in Education Policy

We frame this chapter in a grab-bag of theoretical resources including social constructionism and the notion of capability, and their joint impact on policy effects. The term *social constructionism*, which gained considerable popularity since the publication of Berger and Luckmann's 1966 book *The Social Construction of Reality: A Treatise in the Sociology of Knowledge,* is the notion that nothing is fixed or predetermined because previously unquestioned certainty can change through one's involvement in social contexts. These include rules, norms, laws or principles of forming and reforming (Coghlan & Brydon-Miller, 2014). The concept of social constructionism holds that the learning process requires dialogue in social situations; in other words, learning involves more than one person and it occurs during social interactions between individuals. Social interaction involves assumptions and negotiation, which results in constructed learning. In relation to the impact of this theoretical position on learning, Burr (2003) states "social constructionism insists that we take a critical stance toward our taken-for-granted ways of understanding the world, including ourselves" (p. 2). It instead challenges us to view knowledge as something that is constructed through interaction with other people (Corcoran, 2017). Social constructionism does not produce one fixed definition nor does it necessarily consider divisions of a topic. Moreover, social constructionism develops over time. Therefore, how knowledge is socially constructed by people and their culture influences their practices and in turn how they understand how the world operates.

In relation to giftedness and twice-exceptionality, it might be argued that it is itself a construct that has been influenced arbitrarily by social constructionism (O'Connor, 2012). Supporting this view, Borland (2003) states that giftedness is not a fact of nature but a social construction. Emphasising the social, Wong (2017) adds that giftedness is a construct that is based on a person's knowledge, experiences and the contexts they are in – that is an invented way of categorising children. Pfeiffer (2013) also comments that every culture has used the concept of giftedness as a label to explain and recognise children who perform exceptionally well in different areas of the domains that that culture values.

Regarding contemporary education, Schulz (2005) explains that education has become competitive because a person's success is determined by their achievements. Success and the achievements that are valued, however, are defined by the social system in which the person lives because the concept of meritocracy is adjusted by the social group's view of which talents or abilities are important and may benefit society (Wong & Morton, 2017). Thus, the notion of meritocracy creates emphasised values of success.

Key to this analysis is the social construction of capability in policy, and the subsequent material effects of specific policy discourse on the education of children labelled as gifted and/or 2E. Seeking to critically evaluate the social justice intent of policy, Gale and Molla (2015) draw on Amartya Sen's (1985) approach to theorising capability as a device of substantiative opportunity rather than the utilitarian sum of resources. Sen's thesis holds that people's capability ought to be evaluated through the freedoms that they have to choose, rather than the resources they possess, or their own estimation of satisfaction. Following Sen's characterisation of capability evaluation to explore how the notion appears in contemporary education policy and curriculum (Australian Government, 2012); Australian Curriculum, 2013), Gale and Molla note that overtaking notions of social justice and wellbeing, capability appears to have been usurped as a notion that represents resource accumulation, or merit. Capabilities directly relevant to the requirements of industry include learning outcomes of generic and specific knowledge and skills of key subject areas, rather than substantiative freedoms. Consequently, "actual policy arrangements focus on the distribution of resources…rather than ensuring students' choices and improving their experiences in curricular and pedagogical aspects of the education process" (p. 818).

Along similar lines, gifted and 2E children are characterised in policy as having expanded capabilities in either academic, sporting, artistic, technical, creative, or social pursuits, to which education providers ought to respond (Ministry of Education, 2012; Parliament of Victoria, 2014). While capability to this end is not an accurate measurement of social justice, its utility lies in its expanded definition. Beyond merely increasing curriculum access to gifted students in one or more of these highlighted skills, "capability through education underscores the value of education for achieving skills and knowledge that generate socio-economic benefits, including better employment opportunities, improved levels of health, active civic participation, and recognition and reward" (Gale & Molla, 2015, p. 818).

How capability of gifted and 2E children appears in the policy documents that we explore in this chapter responds to Terzi's concern (2014) that policy and pedagogy of inclusive schooling is disputed territory. Regarding the identification of giftedness, different constructs of giftedness all include some elements about learning differences as well as recognition that some children have advanced abilities. Yet despite the definitions of giftedness being changeable, whether a child is gifted or not is often determined through the use of narrowly-structured identification tools, such as IQ tests, school reports and observations (Moltzen, 2011).

The term gifted is used in psychological and educational contexts to describe highly capable children, yet Borland (1997) states that giftedness is not only a construct but also a construction. By this, Borland means that giftedness is a concept that people have constructed or invented through conversation. The analysis that we present later in this chapter shows the tensions present in educators' and parents' capacity to define giftedness, alongside those definitions outlined in education policy documents. That giftedness is not a fact of nature or something that educators and psychologists have discovered is evident in the way definitions of giftedness are dynamic. Before presenting the analysis of data to this end, we first need to explore how policy constructs capability among gifted learners to consider its impact on the enactment of educational programs.

4 Giftedness as Constructed by New Zealand's Ministry of Education and the Victorian Parliament

In this chapter we analyse three resources published by the New Zealand Ministry of Education and one by the Parliament of Victoria. Our objective is to show how policymakers have constructed giftedness and twice-exceptionality

and how these constructions are implicit in the discrepancies that manifest between schooling practices and parents' experiences. The four resources are:
- *Gifted and talented students: Meeting their needs in New Zealand schools* (2000);
- *Initiatives for gifted and talented learners* (2002);
- *Gifted and talented students: Meeting their needs in New Zealand schools* (2nd ed.) (Ministry of Education, 2012); and
- Aiming High – A strategy for gifted and talented children and young people 2014 – 2019 (DEECD, 2014).

At this point we wish to note that although we use the term gifted and talented throughout this chapter, we do so simply because of its routine appearance in these publications; our use of the term does not signal our endorsement of it.

The rationale behind the first publication, *Gifted and talented students: Meeting their needs in New Zealand schools* (2000) (hereafter shortened to *Meeting their needs*) was twofold: to raise awareness of potentially unrecognised giftedness and talents among children, and to support the development of educational programmes that could meet their specific learning needs. Building on this initial action, the Ministry of Education established a working party in May 2001 to further develop a policy for gifted education, and *Initiatives for gifted and talented learners* (hereafter shortened to *Initiatives*) was published in 2002. This booklet is a policy and set of guidelines for schools on how to educate gifted and talented learners. Ten years later, in 2012 the New Zealand Ministry of Education published a 120-page revision of the original document *Meeting their needs*. The reason why these publications were selected for this chapter is because they provide principles that can be used as a framework for all school settings in New Zealand. There are many principles in different sections in *Meeting their needs* (Ministry of Education, 2000), but in *Initiatives* (Ministry of Education, 2002) and the revised edition of *Meeting their needs* (Ministry of Education, 2012) the principles have been consolidated into core principles.

4.1   Principles of the Three New Zealand Ministry of Education Documents
The *Initiatives* publication (Ministry of Education, 2002) includes nine core principles to support gifted and talented students, while there are 12 core principles in the revised edition of *Meeting their needs* (Ministry of Education, 2012) that try to cover more diverse perspectives. The latter publication also states that: "Those principles provide a platform on which schools can build their approach to supporting their gifted and talented students more effectively" (p. 15) and "the principles and values laid down in the New Zealand Curriculum call on schools to create curriculums that put students firmly at

the centre of teaching and learning" (p. 54). Both these publications firmly embed gifted and talented education in all aspects of education in Aotearoa New Zealand, although early childhood education is not explicitly mentioned in the 2012 resource.

Initial teacher education and professional development for practicing educators are key components advocated for supporting gifted education in the New Zealand publications. As exemplified in the latter document, teachers need to be supported by "high-quality teacher education and on-going professional learning and development in gifted and talented education" (Ministry of Education, 2012, p. 10). Cultural concepts are also highlighted in the 2012 publication, with the inclusion of one principle based on the Treaty of Waitangi – stating that Māori concepts need to be embraced in the education of gifted and talented students. Differentiated and responsive learning environments are strongly recommended, as are education programmes that include planned progressions, coherent transitions, and clear pathways for gifted and talented students. *Nurturing gifted and talented children* (Ministry of Education, 2008) mentions that giftedness can be found in children from all cultural backgrounds, social classes and disabilities. However, *Meeting their needs* (Ministry of Education, 2012) is the only document that stresses that every gifted and talented student must be provided for, and the document also recognises and embraces students who are twice-exceptional. The Government has also acknowledged that whānau and communities need to work together with schools to support the development of gifted and talented learners. Just as in earlier policies and Government documents, the 2012 gifted and talented education document recommends that teachers be reflective and embed regular self-review in their practice.

5 The approach in Victoria Australia to Gifted Education

Education provision for children and young people identified as gifted and/or 2E has generally differed across Australia, owing to state-based educational governance throughout the country (Jarvis & Henderson, 2014; Plunkett & Kronborg, 2007). Following the release of the Victorian Parliamentary inquiry into gifted education, which identified that a contextualised and coordinated approach to educating gifted and talented learners was lacking across the State, the Victorian Department of Education and Training (Previously Victorian Department of Education and Early Childhood Development) produced the strategic framework 'Aiming High – A strategy for gifted and talented children and young people 2014 – 2019' (Herein Aiming High) (DEECD, 2014). The Strategy develops eighteen initiatives for implementation across the five-year plan designed to ensure a coordinated approach to increasing the learning outcomes of gifted and talented students in Victoria. Notable initiatives within the overall strategy include: streamlining identification procedures with toolkits for parents, early childhood educators and schools; engaging more effectively with families; professional development opportunities for teachers and leadership from early childhood and school settings; supporting transition between education levels and in particular to higher education and post-school options; and continuation of Select Entry Accelerated Learning (SEAL) Programs. Working to support children and families from rural and regional areas, those from disadvantaged backgrounds and diverse cultures are actions emphasised across the strategy.

The strategy (DEECD, 2014) is purportedly all-inclusive of every student across educational sectors in the State of Victoria, and it forms a part of the Government's ten-year plan to become a world leader in learning and development. It aims to do so by supporting gifted and talented learners more holistically, on the basis of their perceived increased capabilities for high achievement. As noted in the strategy report (p. 12): "To become a world leader in education, we must increase the proportion of children and young people performing at the highest levels". The strategy report makes clear that the rationale for its existence is that Victoria has recorded fewer high-level achievements than other OECD jurisdictions. Students labelled gifted, therefore, are anticipated to fill this void by increasing the State's competitive advantage.

6   The Documents' Constructions of Twice-Exceptionality

In *New Zealand, Meeting their needs* recognises that there are some "hidden gifted" children in our education system (Ministry of Education, 2000, p. 33). Students with physical and sensory disabilities and under-achieving gifted and talented students are often in this group. It can be quite difficult to find an indicator of ability if a student is underachieving. The Government suggests that teachers need to observe their students carefully and work with parents. The later revision of *Meeting their needs* (Ministry of Education, 2012) also notes that gifted and talented children with physical and sensory disabilities often under-achieve. The document uses the term twice-exceptional for such children, explaining that "these children are gifted but also have a physical or sensory disability or a learning difficulty. Often their giftedness goes unrecognised because people fail to see past their disability. They can become angry and frustrated and may feel powerless" (Ministry of Education, 2012, p. 10). Gifted children with behavioural difficulties are addressed in another section of the same document: "There is evidence that some gifted students may also have behavioural difficulties such as Attention Deficit Hyperactivity Disorder (ADHD). Other students may have exceptional gifts and talents and also be identified as having an Autism Spectrum Disorder (ASD)" (p. 50).

Our comment is that teachers and professionals have to be very careful when making judgements about gifted and twice exceptional children because, for many parents and teachers, labels can come with negative connotations. Claxton and Meadows (2009) state that how teachers label children who are gifted (or not) negatively influences their view of children. Yet, it has been stated that traditional methods of identification, such as standardised achievement tests, often do not pick up gifted students with learning disabilities because these students' scores are often in the "average" range. Morrison and Horgan (2013) find that twice-exceptional children have challenges to fulfilling their potential. They point out that "the true academic potential of these learners may be overshadowed by their disabilities, or on the other hand, the students' limitations may not be recognised as a consequence of their high achievement" (p. 248). Aiming to increase support for gifted and 2E children on the basis that they are capable, high-achieving students, by implementing such actions like those mentioned in the New Zealand documents, fails therefore to meet these intended goals. Capability is once again limited to the capacity to achieve (Gale & Molla, 2015). We acknowledge that every twice-exceptional student is different – some could perform to an "average" rate for such tests, others could be under-achieving, and some could be uneven in their academic results. Teaching strategies for twice-exceptional students are similar to those that good teachers use with Māori and Pasifika gifted and talented students: paying special attention, and consulting with parents, families and communities (Herewini, Tiakiwai, & Hawksworth, 2012).

In contrast to the New Zealand approach to identification of 2e students, In Victoria Australia, Aiming High (2014) identifies twice exceptional children and young people as those who also have a physical or learning disability. This is framed in the diversity of gifted learners overall, alongside other potential disadvantages including indigeneity, cultural and linguistic diversity, geographical location and low socio-economic backgrounds. The strategy highlights that twice exceptionality may be easily overlooked, and it implies that more responsibility ought to be placed on pedagogical differentiation and educational support for these learners.

7 Identification through Measurement

In New Zealand, identification of giftedness is achieved via a combination of both quantitative and qualitative methods. The documents (Ministry of Education, 2000, 2012) recommend a multi-method approach, as using a variety of methods is more likely to meet the diverse characteristics of students. The two editions of *Meeting their needs* (Ministry of Education, 2000, 2012) include detailed explanations of the principles of identification. The first edition has eight core principles of identification of gifted and talented children (Ministry of Education, 2000, p. 27). To summarise, these include the principle that identification of giftedness includes an on-going measurement of progress. Teachers also need to be aware of hidden giftedness and underrepresented groups, and use a multi-method approach with open communication with those who are working with or close to the child. It is noteworthy that more principles for identification of gifted and talented children appear in the revised 2012 edition of *Meeting their needs* than in the original published in 2000. Another new principle in the 2012 document is about staff needing professional development to learn about and how to implement processes for identifying giftedness.

In Victoria Australia, Aiming High (Parliament of Victoria, 2014) recognises that identification of giftedness is complex. The document cautions teachers not to make assumptions about students who might be gifted based on preconceived ideas of age, disability, socio-economic background or cultural and linguistic diversity. In so doing they acknowledge that giftedness is constructed differently in diverse cultures. The document recommends observation of students to qualitatively apprehend if they might be exhibiting initial characteristics of giftedness. On this note they recommend close collaboration with families.

In both country contexts, teachers need to consider the reliability and validity of available tools of identification, as well as the appropriateness of their use for the context of the child. For example, *Meeting their needs* (Ministry of Education, 2012) states that the scales are designed for middle primary schools or onwards, and cultural understandings and beliefs may also affect the reliability and validity of the results.

Before continuing this analysis, the following section provides a detailed description of how the data of Mel's PhD project has been collected and how they will be used to further the exploration of the policy documents.

8. The Data Collection Process

A closed Facebook group was created to collect data from parents of gifted or twice exceptional children or young people. The aim behind creating this Facebook group was to capture the participants' experiences and opinions of twice-exceptionality and gifted education. Facebook posts are not limited by location and time, which is one of the benefits of using social media for data collection (Ackland, 2013). As King, O'Rourke, and DeLongis (2014, p. 242) explain, "although researchers have at their disposal a variety of online recruitment methods, social media present unique opportunities for rapid, cost-effective data collection from populations with very specific demographics or interests". Participants from several different countries were recruited to the Facebook group. By the time data collection had been completed in June 2014, the closed Facebook group had 173 members.

Most participants of the study came from the United States and Australia, although there were also many from Canada, Singapore, India and New Zealand. Most were parents of twice-exceptional children, and there were also a few active participants who were early childhood or primary school teachers. At the time of data collection, these teachers taught either in early childhood settings or primary schools. Several teacher educators also contributed to the discussion.

The Facebook group created rich discussion among participants as all questions were posted as open-ended provocations. Once the researcher commenced regular postings of questions, most of the group's members were very keen to participate in on-going discussion. They also exchanged information or shared ideas about how to support their child or students in practice. The children were mostly of preschool and primary school ages. Most of the children attended an early childhood setting or a primary school, although some were being home schooled.

There were many on-going discussions about how teachers and society define and provide for gifted children in educational settings. We present some of these below. Pseudonyms are used in all research material to ensure the anonymity of participants.

9. Findings: Identification, Education, and Measurement of Labelled Children

Analysis of the generated data highlighted that constructions of giftedness are influenced by experiences of teaching and learning, children's interactions with others, and the information parents obtain from the government or other sources. The research also indicated that participants recognised that their constructions were influenced by the history and cultural perspectives of the communities where they lived. A major concern of all participants was how learners with giftedness or twice-exceptionality were identified, educated, and measured against standardised learning outcomes.

An important finding of this study is that a dominant construction of twice-exceptionality in education, like intelligence, is supposedly a physical characteristic that can be measured. It is not surprising then that constructions of twice-exceptionality are often influenced by different tools that are generally associated with the medical model, for example, IQ tests, psychological assessments and standardised tests. Many participants clearly indicated their belief that giftedness has to be "measured" to be able to be defined. This construction relates well to the participants' existing knowledge and experiences. We suggest that the Ministry of Education has influenced this construction as their published documents are commonly used as guidelines for schools and in the wider education system. However Zoe, a parent of a 2E child, expressed how these conceptions limited people's understanding of 2e children: "Giftedness... is a diagnosis of a person who can do certain things – it's not a term I'm comfortable using as it doesn't give justice to the person but has the possibility of being misunderstood or interpreted in a way that is different to who it refers to".

In the past, people often used the phrase '*children who are gifted and disabled (in a specific way)*' to describe children who are twice-exceptional (Wormald et al., 2014). However, twice-exceptionality is emphasised in the construction of giftedness in the latter education guidelines both in Australia (Parliament of Victoria, 2014) and New Zealand (Ministry of Education, 2012). There has been more research published in this area in the last decade (Kay, 2007; Pfeiffer, 2015; Robinson, Shore, & Enersen, 2007; Wormald et al., 2014), and educational professionals are starting to have more conversations about twice-exceptionality. Yet, despite this increased awareness of twice-exceptionality among educators, it is clear that not all teachers recognise and understand the needs of 2e children. For example, Sarah, who joined the Facebook group from Australia and has four children, two of whom are twice-exceptional, wondered in her Facebook post why some teachers do not acknowledge that a gifted child could also have a disability:

> So I was wondering, just because my children are more than capable of doing work set for them, as well as working beyond the standard levels, why would some staff not think that any of them could have any type of learning disorder/disability? 2 of my kids have gone, short of a better

word, wayward – [they have] high anxiety levels, [they] have the fear of failure so on and so on.

Sarah's comments highlight that there is still a need to raise awareness of children's individual learning needs that may or may not be associated with a disability. Many Facebook group participants were familiar with the term twice-exceptionality, possibly because they have experience with children who are gifted and twice-exceptional. Parent Teri defined twice-exceptional as "something that hides their 'gift'". This idea, that giftedness is hidden due to some sort of learning challenge(s), is an interesting response. However, we argue that giftedness is not necessarily hidden – even children who are not identified as twice-exceptional often face learning challenges. When teachers acknowledge and respond to children's needs, they create an effective learning environment that will allow the children's gifts to be shown – whether or not they are formally identified. Teachers need to have strategies and knowledge of how to support twice-exceptional children to achieve goals and overcome challenges throughout the learning process (Sturgess, 2011; Wormald et al., 2014). Willard-Holt, Weber, Morrison, and Horgan (2013) also argue that twice-exceptional children face challenges fulfilling their potential. They point out that "the true academic potential of these learners may be overshadowed by their disabilities, or on the other hand, the students' limitations may not be recognised as a consequence of their high achievement" (p. 248). Supporting this finding, many parents in the Facebook group shared that their child's learning needs and strengths were often not recognised by their teachers.

The comments collected through the research revealed that the communities that participants inhabit held many unfounded assumptions about twice-exceptionality. The constructions of giftedness of many of the Facebook parents included their frustration that the special learning needs of their gifted and/or twice-exceptional child were often not being met and that teachers were more likely to focus on the child's weaknesses than their strengths. As parents, they felt helpless to support their child and there appeared to be no platform available where their voices could be heard. Many of the parents attributed this lack of support for gifted education to teachers and central and local governments. As participants came from several different countries, it is clear that this lack of support is a challenge in Aotearoa New Zealand and beyond.

In terms of identification, teacher Traci was not sure whether twice-exceptionality should be identified and how to go about this if required. She asked: "Should these children be formally identified? Should their learning ability be formally diagnosed? Who should do this and at what age?" Unlike Traci's ambivalent position on formal identification, teacher Ada stated that she would like more support on identification: "It would be helpful to have a specific set of criteria to identify children" and "I think that there needs to be some formal check list/document that helps teachers identify children that may be gifted". Gabel (2005) warns that teachers may experience difficulties balancing definitions of learners' differences, and therefore the medical model is often use to judge children with different labels. Aligning with Gabel's argument, many participants of the Facebook group assumed students would benefit from being identified through scientific methods associated with the medical model. These teachers' constructions of giftedness stood in contrast to each other. Whereas one seemed to beckon for standardised tools to measure giftedness, in contrast, the other teacher appeared to be contented to use observation data, comparing the child with their peers. While standardised tests are probably simpler to use, they are also not necessarily as accurate as they are commonly believed to be, as exemplified by Borland (2003). The apparent uncertainty among teachers about how to measure giftedness has meant that educators who participated in the research used whatever approaches they thought would work for measurement, based on what they know about giftedness.

Mother Jay used her experience as a twice-exceptional learner to criticise the education system's use of standardised measurement of abilities: "It's mass-producing brainwashed citizens. The system supports money and government and not education or learning". This participant did not believe that the system supports fair judgement on student abilities. As she posted, "It [the education system] only gives the perception or veneer of doing such. Also – intelligence is not ability to copy/paste or remember things. We believe it's the ability to adapt and survive in ANY given situation WITHOUT prior knowledge".

Sarah challenged the use of measurement to determine ability:

> Schools have a curriculum they need to follow, and many kids are treated like sheeple [sic], not people....Mostly, those with higher or lower abilities are the ones who suffer. Lower abilities can't keep up, muck up, get punished. Those with higher abilities get bored, which is also punishment.

Sarah's concern is that when the use of standardised measurement dominates the education system, teachers cannot cater for different children's needs.

Eva is concerned that schools buy into standardised testing systems because of funding pressures:

> The only thing taught is how to pass the tests and test-taking strategies so that the school can continue getting funded; that would be very boring for both the teachers and students. Standardised testing has its place but cannot be the end all and be all.

She drew on her own schooling experiences:

> Smart kids will question everything and all authority no matter what. This includes parents and teachers. Perhaps they are now learning to not verbalise the questions, but the questions are still there. In the '70s, there was less reliance on standardised testing than now.

One thing that needs to be pointed out here is that if the construction of giftedness is about measurement associated with the medical model of difference, then education cannot be a fundamental right for all. Florian and Black-Hawkins (2011) state that all students come to school with different needs and abilities, and so no students should be seen as being fundamentally different. However, measurement has become an important construction because society assumes that the medical model of intelligence is to fix, cure or accommodate students (Gabel, 2005).

As exemplified in the above participant dialogues, many limited assumptions about twice-exceptionality were present in education communities. The interpretation of twice-exceptionality is again undertaken by what they know or heard of the patterns of behaviours of these children. These assumptions develop an understanding of learners that is driven by measurement to construct children as 'deficient'. However an alternate construction of a learner, that draws on her/his relationalities with others, with technology and with the self (Goodley & Runswick-Cole, 2016) might be possible. Children who have weaknesses in social and language skills are not necessarily twice-exceptional. The concept of constructing twice-exceptionality is similar to the construction of giftedness; i.e. each of the participants had a construction of the term based on medical models where twice-exceptionality is a physical characteristic that can be measured and what they had observed and/or experienced in their practice, and/or through second-hand information. Connor and Valle (2015) point out that many people mistrust the medical understanding of dis/ability that can prevent, cure and correct children's learning patterns. For those children who seem "unfit" especially those who are underachievers, from a low social class family or different cultures which may cause social problems, schools commonly use "tools" to prepare these children for their experience at school.

10 Discussion: The influence of Ministry of Education Documents on the Construction of Giftedness and Twice Exceptionality

Participants of this research had been influenced by the constructions created by Education policy and its position in supporting gifted education. These documents emphasise functional capabilities, and particularly in New Zealand, make frequent references to measurement to determine intellectual differences. As such, it seems likely that the New Zealand Ministry of Education has had a significant influence on this construction through its publications on giftedness. Due to the strong influence of documents published by the Ministry of Education, teachers see that giftedness can be understood as physical characteristics that can be measured.

Whatever tools are used at schools, the essential purpose is to "cure" students of their conditions. Findings of this study also suggested the Ministry of Education has particular influence on measurement as the significant construction of twice-exceptionality in education. It seems to us that gifted education still needs to be developed in Aotearoa New Zealand in a way that positions it within the realm of inclusive education. The influence of scientific and psychological approaches on gifted education, such as the use of medical models, leads to the overuse of scientific and psychological language that is often found in the education system to divide and label children (Connor & Gabel, 2013). Under these approaches, students who require different kinds of teaching strategies to work within the education system need to rely on people who are trained as professionals whose role is to assess whether or not these children are captured in the bell curve.

Returning to Sen's (1985) conception of Capability, wherein "the conventional utilitarian approach to individuals' advantage and the resources-based evaluation of well-being do not offer a complete framework to evaluate the well-being implications and consequences of social arrangements" (Gale & Molla, 2014, p. 812), demonstrates that the limited construction of giftedness as a capability is restrictive to the project of inclusive education. Instead of capability being understood in Sen's definition as an equality measurement to assess social progress, the constructions of giftedness in gifted education documents in both countries relate more to measurement and identification, which may disadvantage some students. Sternberg (2015) said that tests only sample the children's abilities in the skills they need to meet routine school activities, and there are other skills that simple tests cannot measure and hence identify. He also commented that different types of traditional ability tests and all standardised measurements create problems as some students will inevitably be disadvantaged by such norms-based testing regimes; for example, some students will be placed inside the norms, but others will be placed on the outside.

In other words, the discursive effect of gifted education documents appear to develop an assumption that children who do not fit into the criteria may not have the privilege to receive the support like other gifted children who meet the criteria. These policies and documents have the implied assumption that teachers need to rely on measurement to identify giftedness. However, as demonstrated by the research presented in this chapter, the policies and documents do not fully address individual needs, and even that their use is oppressive because of the influence of the standardised labels generated by the publications.

Within any group of students, there will be a minority who do not learn at the same pace as their peers, and their situation becomes even more challenging if behavioural or social difficulties are a factor. As mentioned earlier, Ministry of Education dedicated to gifted education tend to hold to the belief that giftedness is something real because IQ can be measured. Thus, educational and psychological professionals have tended to focus on measurement of giftedness and labels, rather than exploring ways to practically support gifted children. There appears to have been an assumption, possibly because giftedness has been viewed within a medical framework, that giftedness is something to cure, fix and/or accommodate.

The Ministry of Education's construction of giftedness, along with its recommendations, has strongly influenced people's actions, with the comments from the participants in this chapter showing that they rely on measurement to determine intellectual differences. While the teacher educators did not often talk about measuring giftedness in their interviews, there were many discussions on this topic among the Facebook participants. In particular, the parents in the Facebook group talked about their experiences at school in relation to measuring their child's abilities and provision for giftedness based on the outcomes of such measurements. The parent participants reported that they feel they have to listen to and follow the advice of those who are professionals, and that they, the parents, become powerless in any decision making in their child's learning.

Illustrated by a capability perspective that "a person's life is a combination of various doings and beings, and understanding the quality of a person's life requires assessing the substantive freedoms to choose the life he or she has reasons to value" (Gale & Molla, 2015, p. 812), leads us to conclude that the limited notions of capability in the New Zealand Ministry of Education documents and to some extent in the Parliament of Victoria's intervention, do not provide for authentic freedoms to meeting individual learning needs. To implement a more inclusive framework that relies on a broadened definition of capability, As Terzi (2014) advances, should seek to acknowledge individual capacity and effective opportunities for functioning. Such a view of equity could achieve inclusive activities in learning environments. This might also support students to have freedom to feel valued by their teachers.

11   Conclusion

This chapter has explored policies in New Zealand and Victoria Australia that focus on educational provision to children and young people labelled gifted or twice-exceptional (Ministry of Education, 2000, 2010, 2012; Parliament of Victoria, 2014). Research participants shared their experiences of being labelled as gifted and twice-exceptional, which led to some feeling purposely marginalised from full participation in learning environments. Data were collected for this qualitative project via a closed Facebook group that facilitated discussion with parents of children labelled either gifted or twice-exceptional, as well as some educators. The data presented in this chapter have highlighted that measurement is a factor in the construction of giftedness for many people, a finding that implies that capability can be judged as a physical characteristic. The data show that each participant has a personal construction which has evolved over time with experience and new knowledge. The research participants have told us that intelligence, and hence giftedness, is being measured in many different ways in schools and early childhood settings, both in New Zealand, Australia and overseas. Thus, the data illustrated how teachers create different constructions, and that these constructions are influenced by government documents.

Building on this work, this chapter addressed how policy positions in both countries construct giftedness and/or twice-exceptionality. These constructions consequently impact on the school experiences of children and their families. The study discovered that narrow definitions of capability influenced parents' concerns about the learning environments and the competitiveness of schools for the impact this had on their children's education. The conclusion from this analysis is that narrow conceptions of capability, as made possible by reductive measurements of giftedness, are detrimental to the inclusiveness of education.

References

Ackland, R. (2013). *Web social science: Concepts, data and tools for social scientists in the digital age.* Thousand Oaks, CA: Sage Publications.

Berger, P. L., & Luckmann, T. (1966). *The social construction of reality: A treatise in the sociology of knowledge*. Garden City, NY: Doubleday.

Borland, J. H. (1997). The construct of giftedness. *Peabody Journal of Education, 72*(3–4), 6–20. doi:10.1207/s15327930pje7203&4_1

Burr, V. (2003). *An introduction to social constructionism*. New York, NY: Routledge.

Claxton, G., & Meadows, S. (2009). Brightening up: How children learn to be gifted. In T. Balchin, B. Hymer, & D. Matthews (Eds.), *The Routledge international companion to gifted education* (pp. 3–9). New York, NY: Routledge.

Coghlan, D., & Brydon-Miller, M. (Eds.). (2014). *The Sage encyclopedia of action research* (Vols. 1–2). London: Sage Publications.

Connor, D. J., & Gabel, S. L. (2013). "Cripping" the curriculum through academic activism: Working toward increasing global exchanges to reframe (dis)ability and education. *Equity & Excellence in Education, 46*(1), 100.

Connor, D. J., & Valle, J. W. (2015). A socio-cultural reframing of science and dis/ability in education: Past problems, current concerns, and future possibilities. *Cultural Studies of Science Education, 10*(4), 1103–1122. doi:10.1007/s11422-015-9712-6

Corcoran, T. (2017). Ontological constructionism. In A. Williams, T. Billington, D. Goodley, & T. Corcoran (Eds.), *Critical educational psychology* (pp. 26–33). Oxford: John Wiley & Sons.

Davidson, J. E. (2009). Contemporary models of giftedness. In L. V. Shavinina (Eds.), *International handbook on giftedness* (pp. 81–95). Dordrecht: Springer.

Department of Education and Early Childhood Development (Victoria) (DEECD). (2014). *Aiming high: A strategy for gifted and talented children and young people 2014–2019*. Melbourne: Author.

Florian, L., & Black-Hawkins, K. (2011). Exploring inclusive pedagogy. *British Educational Research Journal, 37*(5), 813–828. doi:10.1080/01411926.2010.501096

Gabel, S. L. (2005). *Disability studies in education* (Vol. 3). New York, NY: Peter Lang.

Gale, T., & Molla, T. (2014). Social justice intents in policy: An analysis of capability for and through education. *Journal of Education Policy, 30*(6), 810–830. doi:10.1080/02680939.2014.987828

Goodley, D., & Runswick-Cole, K. (2016). Becoming dishuman: Thinking about the human through dis/ability. *Discourse: Studies in the Cultural Politics of Education, 37*(1), 1–15. doi:10.1080/01596306.2014.930021

Herewini, L., Tiakiwai, S.-J., & Hawksworth, L. (2012). Gifted and talented. *Set: Research Information for Teachers, 2*, 41–48.

Jarvis, J. M., & Henderson, L. (2014). Defining a coordinated approach to gifted education. *The Australasian Journal of Gifted Education, 23*(1), 5–15.

Jarvis, J. M., & Henderson, L. (2015). Current practices in the education of gifted and advanced learners in South Australian schools. *The Australasian Journal of Gifted Education, 24*(2), 70–86.

Kay, K. (2000). *Uniquely gifted: Identifying and meeting the needs of twice-exceptional students.* Gilsum, NH: Avocus Pub.

King, D. B., O'Rourke, N., & DeLongis, A. (2014). Social media recruitment and online data collection: A beginner's guide and best practices for accessing low-prevalence and hard-to-reach populations. *Canadian Psychology, 55*(4), 240.

Long, L. C., Barnett, K., & Rogers, K. (2015). Exploring the relationship between principal, policy, and gifted program scope and quality. *Journal for the Education of the Gifted, 38*(2), 118–140.

Ministry of Education. (1996). *The Whariki: He whariki matauranga mo nga mokopuna o Aotearoa: Early childhood curriculum.* Wellington: Learning Media.

Ministry of Education. (2000). *Gifted and talented students: Meeting their needs in New Zealand schools.* Retrieved from http://gifted.tki.org.nz/

Ministry of Education. (2002). *Initiatives in gifted and talented education.* Wellington: Ministry of Education.

Ministry of Education. (2008). *Nurturing gifted and talented children: A parent-teacher partnership.* Wellington: Learning Media.

Ministry of Education. (2012). *Gifted and talented students: Meeting their needs in New Zealand schools.* Retrieved from http://gifted.tki.org.nz/

Moltzen, R. (2011). *Gifted and talented: New Zealand perspectives.* Auckland: Pearson.

National Association for Gifted Children. (2010/2011). *State of the nation in gifted education.* Retrieved from https://www.valdosta.edu/colleges/education/psychology-and-counseling/documents/state-of-the-nation-10.pdf

O'Connor, J. (2012). Is it good to be gifted? The social construction of the gifted child. *Children & Society, 26*(4), 293–303.

Parker, L. (2015). Critical race theory in education and qualitative inquiry: What each has to offer each other now? *Qualitative Inquiry, 21*(3), 199–205. doi:10.1177/1077800414557828

Pfeiffer, S. I. (2013). *Serving the gifted: Evidence-based clinical and psychoeducational practice.* New York, NY: Routledge.

Pfeiffer, S. I. (2015). Gifted students with a coexisting disability: The twice exceptional. *Estudos de Psicologia (Campinas), 32*(4), 717–727.

Plunkett, M., & Kronborg, L. (2007). Gifted education in Australia: A story of striving for balance. *Gifted Education International, 23*(1), 72–83.

Robinson, A., Shore, B. M., & Enersen, D. L. (2007). *Best practices in gifted education: An evidence-based guide.* Waco, TX: Prufrock Press.

Sen, A. (1985). Well-being, agency and freedom: The Dewey lectures. *Journal of Philosophy, 82*(4), 169–221.

Sternberg, R. J. (2015). Successful intelligence: A model for testing intelligence beyond IQ tests. *European Journal of Education and Psychology, 8*(2), 76–84. doi:10.1016/j.ejeps.2015.09.004

Sturgess, A. (2011). Celebrating the square peg: Twice-exceptional learners. In R. Moltzen (Ed.), *Gifted and talented: New Zealand perspectives* (3rd ed., pp. 379–403). Auckland: Pearson.

Terzi, L. (2014). Reframing inclusive education: Educational equality as capability equality. *Cambridge Journal of Education, 44*(4), 479–493.

Willard-Holt, C., Weber, J., Morrison, K. L., & Horgan, J. (2013). Twice-exceptional learners' perspectives on effective learning strategies. *Gifted Child Quarterly, 57*(4), 247–262. doi:10.1177/0016986213501076

Winebrenner, S. (2003). Teaching strategies for twice-exceptional students. *Intervention in School and Clinic, 38*(3), 131–137.

Wong, M. (2017). Constructing giftedness: Discursive texts of teacher educators. In M. Wong (Ed.), *Rethinking research with practice: Multiple perspectives for early years education*. Auckland, New Zealand: Manukau Institute of Technology. Retrieved from https://indd.adobe.com/view/fb942b3f-df5c-4e42-8bef-db93d99f0e5d

Wong, M., & Morton, M. (2017). Parents' lived experiences of teachers' construction of giftedness: Is meritocracy part of the problem? In V. Plows & B. Whitburn (Eds.), *Inclusive education: Making sense of everyday practice*. Rotterdam, The Netherlands: Sense Publishers.

Wormald, C., Vialle, W., & Rogers, K. (2014). Young and misunderstood in the education system: A case study of giftedness and specific learning disabilities. *The Australasian Journal of Gifted Education, 23*(2), 16–28.

CHAPTER 7

Employing Intersectionality and the Concept of Difference to Investigate Belonging and Inclusion

Leechin Heng and Julie White

1   Introduction

In this chapter, we outline a theoretical framework for thinking further about belonging and inclusion by considering the potential of intersectionality theory and the concept of difference. How the simultaneous effects of race, class, ethnicity, gender, citizenship status, disability and categorisation impact on marginalised subjectivities, and how this fits within inclusive discourses is of interest here. The purpose of this chapter is to contribute to equity scholarship by proposing how theory might help us to think about inclusion differently. While the terms 'belonging' and 'inclusion' often assume the notion of joining the mainstream, this presupposes a 'norm' into which something or someone has to belong or be included into.

This chapter investigates how belonging and inclusion might be otherwise reconstructed by employing theory that serves to frame the discourse differently. We attempt to employ theoretical approaches that may be useful for reconsidering the harmful effects of the categorisation of people into hierarchies and instalments. Many people do not fit white, straight, middle-class, gendered norms. By drawing upon the theory of intersectionality and the concept of difference, we investigate and challenge ideas about fixed identities and how inclusion works. The concept of difference (Grosz, 2011) and intersectionality theory are examined to determine how discussion about inclusion can be advanced beyond the idea that it is about "bringing in" (Graham, 2006, p. 20). Because "to include is not necessarily to *be* inclusive" (Graham & Slee, 2006, p. 3, emphasis in the original). The idea that inclusion "presupposes a whole into which something (or someone) can be included" (Graham & Slee, 2006, p. 4) is also challenged in this chapter.

The chapter begins with a detailed exploration of intersectionality – as theory, paradigm and as methodology. This is followed by an examination of the concept of difference. The chapter then turns to examine how intersectionality and the concept of difference might work interactively to assist the inquiry process within inclusion discourses.

2   Intersectionality

Intersectionality has been variously described as a theory, a concept, a methodology and an analytical approach. Intersectionality supports consideration of how multiple categories of social group membership, such as race/ethnicity, gender, class, sexuality or disability *jointly* determine experiences and outcomes. Debates in the 1980s about the best way to theorise race, class, gender and sexuality, as well as the substantial increase in theoretical work around race and gender by women of colour, led to increasing attention on intersectionality (Cole, 2009; Brah & Phoenix, 2004; Ferri & Connor, 2010). Developed twenty years ago by feminist and critical race theorists, the groundwork for intersectionality emerged from the simultaneous positioning of women as also black, working class, lesbian or colonial subjects (Phoenix & Pattynama, 2006). Crenshaw (1989), a legal scholar, is credited with coining the term, although other scholars were also concurrently drawing attention to the limitations of analyses that isolated race or gender as the primary category of identity, difference, or disadvantage (Cole, 2009). Yuval-Davis (2006) stresses that the purpose of using intersectionality is to unpack the ways in which political and subjective constructions of identities work to create the 'other', rather than as a one-size-fits-all social category to put all those as having been politically and subjectively constructed as 'others' into.

Intersectionality has attracted critique from many quarters, but as Tomlinson (2013) notes, much of it relies on a patterned and discipline-based argument that doesn't take us far. While acknowledging specific difficulties within intersectionality research, Nash (2008) nevertheless provided early encouragement to grapple with intersectionality's 'murkiness' in order to consider more complex ways of theorizing identity and oppression. Puar (2013) also draws attention to difficulties with intersectionality and proposes a re-reading of intersectionality that incorporates assemblages while Fotopoulou (2012) suggests hybridity as a complementary methodological approach to intersectionality and queer studies. In arguing for a field of intersectionality studies, rather than more definitions or dismantling of intersectionality, Cho, Crenshaw, and McCall (2013) outline some of the complex and contested ways intersectionality has been employed. They suggest that intersectionality has potential to be developed, theoretically and practically, within interdisciplinary study concerned with inequality. McCall (2008) argues that despite research practice mirroring the complexity of social life, little is revealed in the literature about how to use intersectionality in research.

3   Intersectionality as Theory

Crenshaw's (1991) emphasis on black women's experience of identity and oppression locates intersectionality as a theory of *marginalised subjectivity*. She argues that "the ways in which the location of women of colour *at the intersection of race and gender* makes [their] actual experience of domestic violence, rape and remedial reform qualitatively different from that of white women" (p. 3, emphasis added). In a discussion of Crenshaw's pioneering legal scholarship on the intersection of gender and race, Verloo (2006) raised the question, "How and when does racism amplify sexism?" (p. 213). This question identifies the doubling, or compounding, nature of complexity and oppression, and the point of intersectionality. Furthermore, Yuval-Davis (2006) notes that class is an additional category in the oppression of Black women, as in the notion of 'triple oppression': race/ethnicity, class and gender.

Gillborn (2015)'s highly influential study highlights the effects of race, gender and class have on assuming incompetence on students' disability. Ferri and Connor (2014) note that little is acknowledged on how "social and economic inequality, like race, influence both dis/ability classification and the outcomes associated with various dis/ability designations" (p. 472). It should be noted, however, that Yuval-Davis (2006) criticises this notion of triple oppression, noting that "in such identity politics construction, what takes place is actually fragmentation and multiplication of the wider categorical identities, rather than the more dynamic, shifting and multiplex constructions of intersectionality" (p. 195). Yuval-Davis (205) stresses that the aim of intersectionality is to critically analyse and situate where and how social divisions that constructs some identities as 'other', that has the potential for them to be treated as less or inferior.

Intersectionality as theory therefore allows for attention to be paid to the complex interaction of individual histories and connections, such as race, class, ethnicity, gender and disability, which play out as compounding inequalities (Annamma, Connor, & Ferri, 2016). Additionally, intersectionality stresses the interwoven nature of oppressive categories, and how they strengthen or weaken each other (Crenshaw, 1989; Winker & Degele, 2011). It offers the potential to make visible the multiple positionings that constitutes everyday life and the power relations that are central to it (Phoenix & Pattynama, 2006, p. 187). At the centre of intersectionality is a vision of equality. It seeks to foreground those whose experiences and subjectivities have until now been ignored. (Nash, 2008).

4   Intersectionality as Research Paradigm

Hancock (2007) asserts that intersectionality should be seen as a research paradigm, rather than merely a content specialisation, particularly in the conduct of empirical research with populations with intersecting marginalised identities. As she notes, "intersectionality as a research paradigm can generate problem-driven research: it takes a problem in the world, analyses and moves beyond earlier approaches to studying the problem, and develops a more powerful model to test its effectiveness in addressing the problem" (p. 75). Specifically, it involves a shift from having categories of investigation determined *a priori* to one of empirical investigation where reductive and static categories like race or gender are challenged. As Ybema, Yanow, Wels, and Kamsteeg (2010) emphasise, the world does not "arrive pre-labelled and pre-theorized" (p. 8). Intersectionality thus allows us to identify the hegemonic, structural, disciplinary and interpersonal playing fields upon which race, class, gender, disability and other categories of difference interact to produce society. It also allowed us to explore the covert and overt, the private troubles and public issues (Mills, 1970), the challenges and implications, the excitement and complexities, in which the social world functions.

In a similar vein, Cole (2009) argues that intersectional analysis requires a conceptual or paradigm shift about how socially constructed categories are understood by researchers; it offers a way to conduct research related to social issues, public policy and practice in a theoretical manner. Cole suggests that researchers using the concept of intersectionality as theory and methodology ask the following three research questions that allow for multiple layers of intersectional inquiry: Who is included within this category? What role does inequality play? Where are the similarities? By asking these three questions, categories such as race, gender or disability are viewed as *structural categories* and *social processes* rather than individual characteristics, making it possible to identify the mechanisms by which the different categories intersect to produce difference and disadvantage, and allowing researchers to approach these intersections in a theoretical way. Cole (2009) further explains that intersectionality serves to break away the tendency to view categories in essentialist terms rather than looking for who to 'include' or who has yet to be 'included'.

As such, paying attention to those who have been traditionally excluded in research allows for a contextualised and nuanced understanding of experiences (as opposed to viewing groups in the ways they differ from dominant groups), and the identification of multiple identities that define privilege, such as middle-class status, heterosexuality, able-bodiedness and whiteness. Further, it allows for the investigation of the ways social categories *structure* individual and social life. Cole notes that categories such as race, gender, social class sexuality and disability "encapsulate historical and continuing relations of political, material, and social inequality and stigma and multiple category memberships position individuals and groups in asymmetrical relation to one another, affecting their perceptions, experiences and outcomes" (p. 173).

5 Intersectionality as Methodology

While the concept of intersectionality as theory and research paradigm is well understood, the challenge for researchers is the development of research designs and methods that effectively capture the tenets of intersectionality as a theory. Hancock (2007) notes that the idea of analysing race, class and gender identities together has existed for more than a century. While some have taken a unitary approach, that is, consideration of only one category at a time, others have taken a multiple or additive approach, as in the gradual incorporation of race in gender studies. However, Hancock criticises both these approaches; instead, she advocates for an intersectional approach which answers questions that are left unanswered by unitary and multiple approaches (p. 71). She defines intersectionality as both theory and methodology, that is, as referring to "*both* a normative theoretical argument *and* an approach to conducting empirical research that emphasises the interaction of categories of difference (including, but not limited to race, gender, class, and sexual orientation)" (pp. 63–64, emphasis in the original). Furthermore, intersectionality posits that the interactive, mutually constitutive relationships among categories shape political institutions, political actors, the relationships between institutions and actors, as well as the categories themselves. Intersectionality theory proposes that multiple marginalisations – at both individual and institutional levels – create social and political stratification, such that policy solutions need to be attuned to these categories. As Hancock emphasises, "policy problems are more than the sum of mutually exclusive parts; they create an interlocking prison from which there is little escape" (p. 65). Ferri and Connor (2014) observe that the privileged claim of ability or normalcy are denied for people who are disadvantaged by social economic status (SES). They further state that "ability as property" (p. 472) is used to justify segregation and perpetuate marginalisation for already marginalised groups. Inequality associated with social class is so powerful that it is hard for any institution to mitigate such social inequities.

Nash (2008) argues that intersectional theory should look at race and gender, not only as categories, but also as social processes that inform each other but operate in different ways. Intersectionality highlights that race, class, ethnicity, gender and dis/ability are lived in, through and sometimes alongside each other (Ferri & Connor, 2014). Nash (2008), drawing from McCall (2005), characterises intersectionality as a multidisciplinary approach to analysing the individual experience of both identity and oppression. Nash also notes that intersectionality is a tool which has the potential to respond to critiques of identity politics by demonstrating that "racial variation(s) within gender and the gendered variation(s) within race through its attention to subjects whose identities contest race-or-gender categorizations" (pp. 2–3). Citing Wing (1990) and Matsuda (1990), Nash emphasises the need for intersectionality to be able to conceptualise identity so as to capture the ways in which categories such as race, gender, class, and sexuality "are produced through each other, securing both *privilege* and *oppression* simultaneously" (p. 10, emphasis added), as well as the ways in which privilege and oppression intersect to inform each subject's experiences. Finally, Nash conceptualises intersectionality as a "tool for excavating the voices of the marginalized" (p. 13).

6   Concept of Difference

Unlike intersectionality, the concept of difference is not a theory or a research paradigm. Concept is a way in which, "the living adds ideality to the world, transforming the givenness of chaos, the pressing problem, into various forms of order, into possibilities for being otherwise" (Grosz, 2011, p. 89). Theorists including Foucault, Derrida, Deleuze and Guattari have problematised and critiqued how research often marginalises certain knowledge and held Western ideology as superior (St. Pierre, 2013). Bell hooks (1994) stresses that traditional teacher education curriculum is based on such Western ideology and this ideology is universally transmitted to pre-service teachers.

Concepts are tools that enable ways in which to deconstruct, recognise and acknowledge that knowledge is not innocent and definitely not outside power relations. As Grosz points out, "Knowledges are weapons, tools, in the struggles of power over what counts as truth, over what functions as useful, over what can be used to create new systems, forces, regimes, and techniques, none of which are indifferent to power" (p. 87). Braidotti (2013) argues that *normality*, *normalcy* and *normativity* underpin what is dominantly constructed as the *human norm*. This makes human beings self-regulatory and instrumental to practices of exclusion and discrimination without themselves being aware of it.

In the context of our work about belonging and inclusion, we aim to highlight different ways of knowing and that truths exist in multiple ways. Rather than asking questions such as, 'How can we include marginalised and oppressed groups into the norm?' The concept of difference instead asks: 'How can we transform the norm?' So that differences "do *not* emerge and function only through the suppression and subordination of other social identities?" (Grosz, 2011, p. 99, emphasis in original).

7 Intersectionality and Concept of Difference: Meeting at the Crossroad

Intersectionality is not about looking at how various marginalised groups are oppressed, but rather it asks for a paradigm shift in focusing at the core of how marginalised groups are constructed to be inferior or "a commitment to consider different orders of things, different *distributions*, that have been and might be" (St. Pierre, 2014, p. 14). Arguments against this approach may be threatening, unwelcomed, or even seemed accusatory, to groups whose identity, or sense of belonging, is attached to their relationship to their identity, for example, in the case of the Deaf community, which has often identified itself as linguistically different, rather than as a disability or marginalised group. These communities disassociate themselves from disability or marginality. The importance of intersectionality theory and the concept of difference for our investigation of belonging and inclusion does not intend to disregard differences. Instead it aims to develop alliances to challenge discriminatory discourses that construct differences as deviant.

Grosz (2006) reminds us that problems coexist with solutions and what may appear to be 'problems' can also be opportunities for change. As Braidotti (2013) asserts, deconstructing the frames that prevent inclusion from being inclusive need not lead to despair, but it can be an affirmative process. Braidotti stresses that instead of identifying hopelessness in the past and present, we need to look at what possibilities might emerge from oppressive and discriminatory practices. Ahmed (2007) claims that terms such as 'equity', 'belonging' and 'inclusion' are often over used, resulting in institutional policies proclaiming to be 'equitable' and 'fair'. Ahmed notes the paradox of this usage and repetition, but the failure to act. Ahmed comments that this emancipatory terminology becomes outdated and weighed down by its own inaction and people tire of hearing it.

Therefore, we use intersectionality and the concept of difference to think about what could change. Focusing on the past is a useful means of finding possibilities, not an end in itself. Social science research has tended to lay the blame for exclusionary practices on social construction (Goodley, Lawthorm, & Runswick-Cole, 2014). Therefore, we propose the theory of intersectionality and the concept of difference as a possible way forward. In order to make greater sense of belonging and inclusion, the concept of difference and may help to develop inclusive thinking and practices. Solutions need to be found amidst the problem.

8 Belonging and Inclusion: Conclusion

The norms presupposed within some inclusion discourses remain cause for concern. This chapter has investigated how belonging and inclusion might be otherwise reconstructed by employing theory that serves to frame these discourses differently. This examination of the concept of difference and intersectionality makes a modest contribution to equity scholarship by proposing how theory might help us to think about inclusion and belonging differently. The idea of belonging, like 'becoming', at first appears to be straightforward, but has been revealed to be deceptively complex. By employing intersectionality and the concept of difference, it is the 'norm' that we seek to challenge and problematise. In this attempt to put intersectionality and the concept of difference to work in reconsidering ideas of belonging and inclusion, our intent is to issue is an invitation to others to reconsider the notions of belonging and inclusion differently.

References

Ahmed, S. (2007). The language of diversity. *Ethnic and Racial Studies, 30*(2), 235–256.

Annamma, S., Connor, D., & Ferri, B. (2016). Dis/ability Critical race studies (DisCrit): Theorizing at the intersections of race and dis/ability. In D. Connor, B. Berri, & S. Annamma (Eds.), *DisCrit: Disability studies and critical race theory in education* (pp. 9–32). New York, NY: Teachers College Press.

Brah, A., & Phoenix, A. (2004). Ain't I a woman? Revisiting intersectionality. *Journal of International Women's Studies, 5*(3), 75–86.

Braidotti, R. (2013). *The posthuman*. London: Polity Press.

Cho, S., Crenshaw, K. W., & McCall, L. (2013). Towards a field of intersectionality studies: Theory, applications, and praxis. *Signs: Journal of Women in Culture and Society, 38*(4), 785–810.

Cole, E. R. (2009). Intersectionality and research in psychology. *American Psychologist, 64*(3), 170–180.

Crenshaw, K. (1989). Demarginalizing the intersection of race and sex: A Black feminist critique of antidiscrimination doctrine, feminist theory, and antiracist politics. *University of Chicago Legal Forum, 140*, 139–167.

Crenshaw, K. (1991). Mapping the margins: Intersectionality, identity politics, and violence against women of color. *Stanford Law Review, 43*(6), 1241–1279.

Ferri, B. A., & Connor, D. J. (2010). 'I was the special ed. girl': Urban working-class young women of colour. *Gender and Education, 22*(1), 105–121. doi:10.1080/09540250802612688

Ferri, B. A., & Connor, D. J. (2014). Talking (and not talking) about race, social class and dis/ability: Working margin to margin. *Race Ethnicity and Education, 17*(4), 471–493. doi:10.1080/13613324.2014.911168

Fotopoulou, A. (2012). Intersectionality queer studies and hybridity: Methodological frameworks for social research. *Journal of International Women's Studies, 13*(2), 19–32.

Gillborn, D. (2015). Intersectionality, critical race theory, and the primacy of racism: Race, class, gender, and disability in education. *Qualitative Inquiry, 21*(3), 277–287. doi:10.1177/1077800414557

Goodley, D., Lawthorm, R., & Runswick-Cole, K. (2014). Posthuman disability studies. *Subjectivity, 7*(4), 342–361.

Graham, L. (2006). Caught in the net: A foucaultian interrogation of the incidental effects of limited notions of inclusion. *International Journal of Inclusive Education, 10*(1), 3–25.

Graham, L., & Slee, R. (2006). *Inclusion?* Paper presented at the American Educational Research Association (AERA) 2006 Annual Conference, San Francisco, CA.

Grosz, E. (2011). *Becoming undone: Darwinian reflections on life, poilitics, and art.* Durham, NC: Duke University Press.

Hancock, A. (2007). When multiplication doesn't equal quick addition: Examining intersectionality as a research paradigm. *Perspectives on Politics, 5*(1), 63–80.

hooks, b. (1994). *Teaching to transgress: Education as the practice of freedom.* London: Routledge.

Matsuda, M. (1990). Beside my sister, facing the enemy: Legal theory out of coalition. *Stanford Law Review, 43*, 1183–1192.

McCall, L. (2005). The complexity of intersectionality. *Signs, 30*(3), 1771–1800.

McCall, L. (2008). The complexity of intersectionality. In E. Grabham, D. Cooper, & D. Herman (Eds.), *Intersectionality and beyond: Law, power and the politics of location.* New York, NY: Routledge.

Mills, C. W. (1970). *The sociological imagination.* Harmondsworth: Penguin.

Nash, J. C. (2008). Re-thinking intersectionality. *Feminist Review, 89*, 1–15.

Phoenix, A., & Pattynama, P. (2006). Editorial: Intersectionality. *European Journal of Women's Studies, 13*(3), 187–192.

Puar, J. (2013). 'I would rather be a cyborg than a goddess': Intersectionality, assemblage, and affective politics. *Meritum, 8*(2), 371–390.

St. Pierre, E. (2013). The posts continue: Becoming. *International Journal of Qualitative Studies in Education, 26*(6), 646–657. doi:10.1080/09518398.2013.788754

St. Pierre, E. (2014). A brief and personal history of post qualitative research: Toward "post inquiry". *Journal of Curriculum Theorizing, 30*, 2–19.

Tomlinson, B. (2013). To tell the truth and not get trapped: Desire, distance, and intersectionality at the scene of the argument. *Signs: Journal of Women in Culture and Society, 38*(4), 995–1017.

Verloo, M. (2006). Multiple inequalities, intersectionality and the European Union. *European Journal of Women's Studies, 13*(3), 211–228.

Wing, A. K. (1990). Brief reflections toward a multiplicative theory and praxis of being. *Berkeley Women's Law Journal, 6*, 181–201.

Winker, G., & Degele, N. (2011). Intersectionality as multi-level analysis: Dealing with social inequality. *European Journal of Women's Studies, 18*(1), 51–66.

Ybema, S., Yanow, D., Wels, H., & Kamsteeg, F. (2010). Ethnography. In A. Mills, G. Durepos, & E. Weibe (Eds.), *Encyclopedia of case study research*. Thousand Oaks, CA: Sage Publications.

Yuval-Davis, N. (2006). Intersectionality and feminist politics. *European Journal of Women's Studies, 13*(3), 193–209.

PART 3
Identity and Well-being – Keys to Belonging

CHAPTER 8

The Impact of Inclusive Education and Access to Sexuality Education on the Development of Identity in Young People Living with Disability

Henrietta Bollinger and Hera Cook

1   Introduction

There is now a cohort of young New Zealanders living with disability whose education has taken place alongside their able-bodied peers in 'mainstream' schools (Dalziel, 2001; Stace, 2015). They have grown into young adulthood with a different sense of themselves and their identity to that of previous generations of disabled New Zealanders. They have new aspirations regarding their rights and identities. This paper reports on a peer research project that undertook indepth interviews with young people with congenital mobility disabilities. The participants were asked to reflect on their experiences of inclusive education in secondary school, specifically in relation to Sexuality Education [SE], and how this informed their post-school experience of, and feelings or beliefs about, embodied sexual activity. It emerged that this related strongly to the impact of mainstreaming on their identity.

2   Theoretical Framework

Many factors contribute to shaping the young disabled person's perception of their potential for romantic and\or sexual relationships. Researchers have found a correlation between the young disabled person's level of social capital and their potential for romantic and sexual relationships. The implication of this for the individual is unclear however, because stigma and stereotypes of asexuality, may limit the ability of others, both able-bodied and disabled, to view their disabled peers as potential romantic or sexual partners (Berman et al., 1999; Wiegerink et al., 2010, 2011). Unsurprisingly, for the disabled person in education, social capital is of the highest value where connections to others affirm and value a disabled identity. In spaces where disability is the exception, negotiating a positive disabled identity is more difficult (Holt, 2010; van Amsterdam et al., 2015) and this tends to privilege the common ground young people share with their able-bodied peers over their disabled identity.

This reinforces the well-documented hierarchy within disability: Kulick and Rydstrom (2015) argue that within this hierarchy, disabled people who are non-verbal and have unknown levels of cognitive function are positioned at the lowest level both socially and in terms of desirability. In this hierarchy, able-bodiness is aspirational, and being as 'normal as possible' is the goal. This has been likened to 'passing' in queer and trans scholarship, and was originally used in relation to racial hierarchies. In this situation, managing competing positive and negative responses to disability requires constant internal negotiation within an often ambivalent self (Campbell, 2009).

Individualization has been the hegemonic societal approach to those living with disability/impairments (Oliver, 1990). A person living with impairments was seen as a victim of personal tragedy and society had no responsibility for the limits on their access to social goods. This was consistent with a medical model according to which normative expectations were applied to disabled people and their bodies were constructed as medical problems that should be fixed by being made to conform as nearly as possible to those of able-bodied people (McLaughlin & Coleman-Fountain, 2014; Shuttleworth, 2007; Thomas, 2004).

The sexual rights and citizenship of people with impairments remain contested and difficult issues and this is reinforced by the issue of dependence and youth. Individuals are permitted a sexual identity when they reach 'adulthood', a state conceived of in terms of becoming independent. This is accompanied by tacit acceptance of sexual activity for pleasure and family formation. Youth is a liminal, transitional category between the categories of 'adult' and 'child' so the sexual citizenship of youth is inherently 'difficult'. In the policing of sexuality, there is debate around the practical and moral issues involved in acknowledging the emergent sexuality of all young people. The level and type of knowledge considered appropriate and the age at which they are permitted to consent to sexual activity are highly contested. The sexual citizenship of youth with disabilities presents a further and even greater challenge to sexual citizenship (Hirst, 2012; Moore, 2013; Robinson, 2012; Richardson, 2000).

The disabled body, and therefore the disabled person, is at odds with the cultural expectation that independence and adulthood are synonymous. A disabled person continues, to a greater or lesser degree, to rely on others to perform tasks, while developing into adulthood with an accompanying adult sexual identity, including needs and desires for intimacy and sexual expression. In light of this assumed, or observed, dependence and its alignment with the infantile, the disabled body, and in turn the person themselves, are rendered ineligible to participate in sexual activity by comparison with the normative, aspirational able-bodied person and body (Kafer, 2003; Mcruer, 2006; McRuer, 2011). The bodies and practices of people living with disability are perceived solely in terms of, or as, limitations according to a construction of independence that privileges non-disabled bodies and their perceived self-sufficiency (Swain & French, 2000).

Disability activists have argued that for people living with impairments, independence may mean the ability to be in control of and make decisions about one's own life, in contrast to an existing definition of independence, as the ability to do things for oneself without assistance from others (Oliver, 1990). This conception of independence can be extended by Gibson, Carnavale, and King's (2012) argument that the negative social connotation of dependence is challenged by postmodern ideas of dynamic connectivity, which offer a different approach to framing the interactions that disabled people have with technologies and caregivers. Gibson (2006) has suggested that 'disability dependencies' on humans, animals and technologies can be reconfigured as "connectivities" that open up possibilities for an altered ethics of the body' in which independence is not privileged as the desired state.

Gibson, Carnavale, and King refer to Donna Harraway's influential *Cyborg Manifesto* (1991), but they, like Oliver, do not address the implications of their ideas for able-bodied people, in this instance, of a fluid understanding of the interconnectedness of human subjectivity and in/dependence among persons, carers and assistive technologies. The situating of disabled people in the classroom, particularly the sexuality education classroom, as dependent, in contrast to able-bodied people who are presumed to be independent, does not reflect the importance of interconnectedness for all embodied human subjectivity. This is especially so in the realm of sexual practice, which is always situated in relation to other/s, even in the instance of solo sexual activity or fantasy. Furthermore, heterosexual sexual practice, as currently experienced, is shaped by and dependent upon on contraceptive and sanitary technologies, to the extent that they operate as assistive technologies (Cook, 2004, 2005). Acknowledgement of the interconnected dependence that is central to all sexual activity has implications for the conception of the disabled body in sexuality education and for a richer understanding of the mutual connectedness and interdependency between bodies that is the foundation of sexual pleasure.

There has now been over a century of pressure to provide positive SE, during which response to such calls has consistently lagged behind change in sexual mores (Cook, 2012). Progressive, feminist and queer SE pedagogy argues that SE must include pleasure, and focus on the self-defined needs of young people rather than the inhibitions and anxieties of older generations (Allen, 2006;

Fine, 2006; Hirst, 2012; Wight, 1999). An inclusive SE classroom in which the disabled body was revalued as sexual, as suggested by affirmative models of disability, would extend these visions of SE by further challenging normative assumptions around what it is to be sexual (Kafer, 2003; Tepper, 2000; Samuels, 2013; Sykes, 2009). This would contribute to creating a SE classroom that is relevant to all young people (Hutchison, 2013).

Thus the social capital of young people living with disability operates within the disability hierarchy. Conceptions of independence and sexual citizenship are defined in ways that mitigate against acknowledgement of interconnectivity and the creation of an inclusive and diverse sexuality classroom from which the discovery of pleasure and agency could be supported.

3   Methods

A central aim of this research project was the inclusion of the voices of young people living with disability. Indepth interviews were used by the peer researcher/interviewer in order to include the voices of young people (East & Orchard, 2013; ERO, 2007). The semi-structured interview schedule included demographic information, schooling, the content and relevance of SE and the negotiation of sexuality, relationships and disability in the interviewees' lives following secondary school (Hansen, 2006). A snowball sample of people living with disability, resident in New Zealand and aged between 18 and 25 years, was obtained via personal connections and advertising on social media.

Ethics approval was granted by the University of Otago Human Ethics Committee and preparations made for potential interviewees with a wide range of disabilities, however, the five young people who participated all had mobility disabilities, the most common disability in this age group (Mcpherson, 2013). Informed consent was sought from participants following an explanation of the research study, clarification that participants were free to withdraw from the study at any time, and assurance that participation was voluntary and anonymous. Support in the event of distress was available for the interviewer and the interviewees. In the event, however the participants and the peer interviewer felt their conversations were personally and socially important and they valued having had the opportunity to discuss their experiences. The interviews were fully transcribed and then coded using NVIVO and thematic analysis (Braun, 2014). In the text, all interview extracts are identified by an interviewee pseudonym.

The sample consisted of three men and two women aged between 21–25 years. Of the five, four had some Christian schooling or identified as Christian.

Maintaining the anonymity of the interviewees who come from a small group within a minority population precluded any analysis of ethnicity. They had attended New Zealand secondary schools alongside their able-bodied peers. Two of the interviewees also had access to an onsite 'unit' or 'Centre' for disabled students at their school and one spent a year in a Special Education unit in another similar country. Four of the participants had received SE through the New Zealand Curriculum. They all had high levels of social capital – as evidenced by supportive families and good networks and they were either studying for, or had already acquired a tertiary qualification. This level of educational achievement is largely new and is, in part, evidence of the success of policy that mandated the integration of people living with disability into 'mainstream' schools in which they are educated beside their able-bodied peers (The Education Act (New Zealand), 1989; Dalziel, 2001). The following discussion describes how 'mainstreaming' has contributed to the construction of a new able/disabled identity and how this is shaping their sexual experience.

4 The Disability Hierarchy and an Able-Disabled Identity

The participants' identities as young academically successful people and their relationship to disabled identity occurred within the context of 'mainstream' schooling. They usually use this term to describe 'regular' schooling, with limited supports alongside their able-bodied peers. In their school life, there was little contact with other disabled people, especially 'high needs intellectually disabled' students. This was evident in a broader distance from their disabled identity. Dave said:

> I, (laughing) this sounds really bad....A lot of the disabled people in my city um were not in mainstream schools and so I didn't want any part of that cause I'd grown up mainstream and that was how I saw myself. Um so probably ninety five per cent of my friends were able bodied.

Dave was reflexive, and self-aware of his attitude towards other disabled people. He offers a disclaimer, 'this sounds really bad', which reveals that he felt apologetic about wanting to distance himself from other disabled people. His own experience of 'being mainstreamed' and 'seeing [himself] that way' means he was aware that disability can be framed positively, yet he did not extend the same normalising frame to those with intellectual\learning disabilities, or to those students not in mainstream schools. Dave was aware of the contradiction of validating his own disabled identity through constructing it as 'normal' while 'othering' the appearance of difference in others.

In this way, Dave touched on the binary construction of ability as either 'able' or disabled. A mainstream student who asserts a strong link to a disabled identity does not fit either of these categories. Disabled students are frequently placed in situations where they are the only person facing the specific adaptive challenges involved in meeting their embodied needs. Negotiating this difference in schools means privileging the common ground these students share with their able-bodied peers over their disabled identity.

The privileging of commonly accepted 'abilities' over an overall positivity about their whole identity means that for these young people the experience of disability is only acceptable where it can be overcome, or does not interfere, with a 'normal' experience of school life. Dave's comments also reveal his experiential support for the disability hierarchy. It is unrealistic to expect disabled people to be immune to such normalizing hierarchies when they are consistently reinforced by the schooling system and social environment, and yet their desire to maintain a distance between themselves and disabled 'others' serves to preserve this hierarchy, which is damaging to the inclusion of all students.

Several interviewees downplayed their use of support services and spaces such as a 'unit' or 'Centre' for disabled students. Carol was the only wheelchair user in her classes. When speaking about support she said 'I went to (the special needs unit) *occasionally* to say hi', though she also used the space on a relatively regular basis for 'exercises'. Accessing a space set aside for people with disabilities had negative connotations for her. She also described the support she received from a teacher aide as 'annoying'. It compromised her perception of herself as 'pretty independent', which was central to her creation of a positive identity. John and Samuel reported the most regular contact with disabled peers. However, even in an environment where disability was the norm, their self-identification with other 'able' identities ensured their experience of being disabled was negative. John, who also faced learning disabilities, found his year in a school for people with disabilities 'rather demeaning, echoing Dave and Carol, by explicitly disassociating himself from students with intellectual disabilities.

Grace asserted particularly quickly that her impairments did not limit her and that disability was normal. In contrast to the other interviewees, Grace's family includes people with her disability raising children and having fulfilling relationships, thus disability was more fully integrated into her identity. She commented: 'Mum and Dad took the opportunity to show friends and relatives (disability) was not a bad thing as such and in doing so encouraged me to be proud of who I am'. Grace had, however, a striking confidence in her 'mainstream' academically successful identity, presenting the 'physical side' as a minor issue. Thus, rather than identifying strongly as disabled, with the partial exception of Grace, the interviewees asserted other identities, focusing on being seen as above average academically and as independent as possible, despite their impairments.

5   Defining Independence

The reach and complexity of the disability hierarchy in these young people's lives is evident in their perception of independence and what this meant for them. The importance of independence in their self-worth implicitly reaffirmed the placement of able-bodied norms at the top of the hierarchy. All the participants saw themselves as independent and this was a central and valued aspect of their identity. Each participant focused on different aspects of independence, however highlighting the areas where they were independent and minimising the presence of supports in their lives. Areas of independence included having moved out of home or having the potential to do so, being self-sufficient with personal care, transport and being able to get from place to place alone. The diverse ways in which the participants drew upon aspects of their lives to present themselves as independent highlighted the importance to them of claiming independence. They all employed their various inclusive understandings of independence to minimize the impact of impairments on their lives. Perhaps most notably, independence was defined in terms of their daily lives in public space and only Samuel mentioned personal care without prompting. Social policy and political energy have been largely focused on self-determination for disabled people in public space and it may be that this has also informed the participant's aspirational ideals of independence.

Underlying all their descriptions but not fully articulated or openly argued for, was a definition of independence similar to Oliver's (1990) 'the ability to be in control of and make decisions about one's life, rather than doing things alone or without help'. In their accounts, they juggled what would be defined as limitations according to the construction of independence which privileges non-disabled bodies and their perceived self-sufficiency. Their capacity and desire to assert their independence is perhaps another outcome of mainstreaming and reflects the fact that they have been given the opportunity to achieve. This should be celebrated, while we also acknowledge the contradictions in their identities as academically and socially able young people living with disability, which aspect of their identity and experience is not acknowledged and valued.

The context for these definitions was a binary opposition of able-bodied independence and disabled, or impaired, dependence that was never questioned. Thus where able-bodied young people are dependent, this is seen as natural and does not compromise their 'independence' (examples include financial dependence into the early twenties, transport support from parents, expectations of emotional support, delay of reproduction). Within a historical framework, a long period of dependence is central to the construction of youth that emerged as part of the ensemble of socio-cultural norms that make up modernity and is central to participation in institutions such as tertiary education. The explosion in recent decades of interconnectedness with devices now considered necessary for able-bodied people of all ages to engage in 'normal' activities and achievements reinforces these earlier changes.

6   Friends

The interviewees had mostly able-bodied friends. Though they were confident in these friendships, often made at school, for the most part their identity as a person living with disability was disregarded rather than shared and affirmed. While many of them felt good about having a 'great group of friends' with whom they founded friendships regardless of 'ability', this meant that the 'successful' areas of their identity were dependent on disengagement from a sense of themselves as people with disabilities and their bodies as impaired. Their disabilities represented a barrier and were largely experienced in their educational and social worlds as negative and stigmatized. Samuel reported 'hating being disabled'. Carol found her disability and the presence of a teacher aide in the classroom disconnected her from her classmates. Unsurprisingly, it has been found that in education the quality of young people's social connectedness is at its best when connections, such as those with friends, teachers and teacher aides, affirm disabled identity (Holt, 2010; Sykes, 2009; van Amsterdam et al., 2015).

Samuel spent most of his time in the mainstream school, only accessing the disability unit for impairment related needs. He felt a 'big divide' between the able-bodied students and students with disabilities, which caused him 'a lot of loneliness'. The other disabled student he mentioned spending time with was, like himself, highly academic. The connection between these two young disabled people highlights the complexity of their rejection of less able disabled young people. On the one hand while they were positive about the belief in social justice that has led to the mainstreaming from which they have benefited, they appear to be accepting societal stigmatisation of disabled people. On the other hand, any implication that academically inclined young people should be friends with others on grounds of shared disability may be to construct them solely as disabled, rather than as multi-faceted people with many other elements to their personality and potential connections leading to the formation of friendships (Holt, 2010).

7 Sexuality Education and Other Information Sources

The participants had a range of sexual aspirations, experiences and desires but they found school SE to be irrelevant to themselves and their bodies, and to their sexuality. The total absence of representations of disabled bodies, or specific support for people living with their disabilities in SE strongly reinforced this attitude, which is, in many respects, shared by able-bodied students who also find SE reinforces stereotypes and is fearful and negative (Allen & Carmody, 2012). This approach undermined the capacity of the participants to discern what might be relevant to them in the SE classroom. In the absence of relevant SE, they had sought out information from other sources.

Four of the interviewees reported they had discussed sexuality with their families. As young children, the response reflected their familial cultures; Carol recalled when she was seven, she asked an older cousin about where babies came from, following which her mother bought her a book about 'how bodies form and stuff (laughing)'. Even though some felt able to be open with their families however, none reported directly discussing their sexuality as disabled people. Samuel said, "my mother was like 'if there's anything you want you can talk to me anytime'. But I'm the only disabled person they know". He felt they would be unable to advise him about sexuality in more than general terms. This perception is supported by the history of parents given the responsibility for SE and finding themselves unable to deliver this effectively either to disabled, or to able-bodied children (Cook, 2012; Kulick & Rydstrom, 2015).

Grace's confidence in her 'mainstream' identity was reinforced by her 'traditional' cultural values, including her Christian belief in 'no sex before marriage'. In contrast to the others, she did not feel she needed classroom SE, rather she believed that where possible these conversations should take place between family and most importantly with her husband to be. She spoke a little about discussing 'relationships generally' with family and trusted friends, however, she did not mention physical sexual activity, the aspect of sexuality which parents (and teachers) find most difficult to discuss with their children.

Other young disabled people are a potential source of sexuality information. Peers have been a major source of information for able-bodied young people (Wellings & Field, 1996). Samuel, John and Dave echoed each other in the need for an 'open channel' to share information between disabled people. 'I can't be the only one who has experienced this', Samuel commented. He felt it would be useful, in particular to talk to other males and had been happy to do so in the past. Dave wanted to tell other young disabled people 'Hey, this...happened for me but it may not happen for you, but it might. This won't happen. This might happen and everything in between. Go have fun'. These impulses were concerned with both seeking support and wanting to give support to others who were younger or less experienced. Conceivably they offer potential for reaching across the disability hierarchy and developing a positive, shared disabled identity.

Expectations of disabled people are changing and Carol recalled a conversation that suggested the limitations in advice from older disabled people. An older woman, who shared Carol's condition, had told her 'not to worry about boys now', when Carol was sixteen and, like her able-bodied friends, interested in dating. This comment made Carol feel 'more asexual', undermining her desire to be acknowledged as a teenager, rather than being defined by her impairment. As she said: 'I was a sixteen year old girl too'. Generational change means older disabled people are likely to feel greater sexual inhibitions that may prevent them from offering appropriate support and information.

In addition, the knowledge that other disabled people have is necessarily limited. Dave was aware that impairment manifested itself very differently in the individual's body even when people had the same condition, citing his own as an example. He felt that speaking to someone else with the same condition could be helpful but was wary of expecting all the answers to come from this source, because of this considerable variation in the condition as it manifested in different individual bodies (Kewman et al., 1997). Excepting for Grace, the interviewees felt there was a need for SE 'personalized' to the particular impact of their disability upon their body. Their able-disabled identity led them to see themselves as independent sexual citizens. From this perspective they believed that medical professionals could provide them with such 'personalized' sexuality information, though none had received this. Medics have frequently felt able to determine the bounds of appropriate behavior despite an absence of training in sexuality or a knowledge base. Thus, medical provision of 'personalized' SE to young disabled people would depend upon new attitudes and increased knowledge (Clare, 2001; Guldin, 2000; Kafer, 2003).

The internet has transformed the availability of information. John, who identifies as gay, had used the internet to inform himself about sex surrogacy and saw this as a potential avenue for sexual expression (Sanders, 2007). Sex work is decriminalized in New Zealand and information about this form of surrogacy is available. Kulick and Rydstrom's (2015) Danish research found that the high costs involved usually put this option out of reach; they found appropriate support to facilitate sexual activity was preferable. It was notable however, that the Danish examples of sex work directly addressed an important issue raised by the interviewees, who found lack of knowledge about their bodies gave rise to a lack of confidence concerning sexual activity; one Danish woman in her late twenties explained that having experienced sexual intercourse with a sex worker gave her confidence in regard to potential partners. John's interest in surrogacy directly highlights the fact that the expectations of young disabled people with an able-disabled identity have the potential to pose a strong challenge to societal inhibitions around the content of SE.

8 Sexuality Education, Sexual Experience

Those who had had sexual and romantic experience at the time of interview found that sex and sexual expression was a highly gendered activity that involved a direct engagement with their bodies as impaired. Their strong 'able', 'mainstream' identities meant that this changing relationship between their able and disabled identities was new and unwanted. The experiences of the male interviewees highlight some of the issues that arose. For Samuel, his level of function compromised his ability to achieve masculine norms: "not saying I'm bad [in bed] but…". Dave felt anxiety about sexual encounters with new partners; he was concerned about 'what the other person might think…of the disability'. And because sex with his disability was 'just different', he had needed knowledge about his body that he did not have.

Carol found she was the last remaining person not in a serious relationship in her immediate [able-bodied] social network; she explained 'it sounds really weird, but I kind of grieved over it for a little while'. Her experience of a sexually active, romantic relationship was, as it is for many young women, disillusioning, but she enjoyed the sexual activity and was glad to have had the experience. So while she commented that 'he definitely took advantage of me like cause I was so vulnerable', her experience cannot be reduced to one of victimization or abuse. Rather Carol felt she had needed knowledge of her body and a conception of herself as an active initiator and negotiator.

Thus, in contrast to Grace, those who wanted, or had experienced, sexual activity, felt it mattered that they were underprepared by school SE. For all of them, sex and sexual expression involved a direct engagement with their bodies as impaired, which was not often their focus as they had strong links to an 'able', 'mainstream' identity. Carol, Dave and Samuel all describe interactions that in varied ways reproduce gendered expectations of women and disabled people as passive, requiring males to be sexually knowing and in control. Grace, in deferring her engagement with sexuality to the future, is able to maintain the assumption that such gendered expectations will serve her well. Research into abstinence education suggests this is frequently not the case (Gardener, 2015). For them all, as for able-bodied students, the SE classroom did not prepare them for the complex, ambivalent emotions their sexual encounters aroused (Lesko, 2010).

9 Conclusion

To summarize, the participants in this research had established independent able-disabled identities but these are undermined when it comes to sexuality because there is no space for their embodied dependence in the existing private and highly gendered model of physical sexual practice. The participants in this study found affirmation and success in areas of school life where disability and impairment could be dismissed as minimal and 'just the physical side'. In these areas they found satisfaction and this was congruent with a positive sense of themselves as able. However, SE and sexual activity required an engagement with their bodies as impaired. The education, and in particular the SE, offered to them failed to make positive space for their entwined identity as both 'able' and 'disabled'.

Mainstreaming provides an opportunity for diverse classrooms that enrich the learning experience of all students, disabled and able-bodied. Progressive, feminist and queer SE pedagogy can be extended to envision an inclusive SE classroom in which the disabled body is revalued as sexual and normative assumptions of what it is to be sexual are challenged. This would contribute to creating a SE classroom that acknowledges the interconnectedness of all sexual activity and could address troubling issues such as emotional exploitation, or lack of confidence in diverse bodies, in a context of trust and support that is relevant to all young people.

References

Allen, L., & Carmody, M. (2012). 'Pleasure has no passport': Re-visiting the potential of pleasure in sexuality education. *Sex Education, 12*(4), 455–468.

Berman, H., Harris, D., Enright, R., Gilpin, M., Cathers, T., & Bukovy, G. (1999). Sexuality and the adolescent with a physical disability: Understandings and misunderstandings. *Issues in Comprehensive Pediatric Nursing, 22*(4), 183–196.

Braun, V., & Clarke, V. (2014). Using thematic analysis in psychology. *Qualitative Research in Psychology, 3*(2), 77–101.

Brisenden, S. (1986). Independent living and the medical model of disability. *Disability, Handicap & Society, 1*(2), 173–178.

Cameron-Lewis, V., & Allen, L. (2014). Teaching pleasure and danger in sexuality education. *Sex Education, 13*(2), 121–132.

Campbell, F. K. (2009). *Contours of ableism: Territories, objects, disability and desire.* London: Palgrave Macmillan.

Clare, E. (2001). Stolen bodies, reclaimed bodies: Disability and queerness. *Public Culture, 13*(3), 359–365.

Cook, H. (2004). *The long sexual revolution: English women, sex and contraception, 1800–1975.* Oxford: Oxford University Press.

Dalziel, L. (2001). *The New Zealand disability strategy: Making a world of difference.* Retrieved from http://www.odi.govt.nz/documents/publications/nz-disability-strategy.pdf

East, L. J., & Orchard, T. R. (2013). 'Why can't I?': An exploration of sexuality and identity among Canadian youth living with physical disabilities. *Journal of Youth Studies, 17*(5), 559–576.

Fine, M. (1988). Sexuality, schooling, and adolescent females: The missing discourse of desire. *Harvard Education Review, 58*(1), 29–54.

Fine, M., & McClelland, S. (2006). Sexuality education and desire: Still missing after all these years. *Harvard Educational Review, 76*(3), 297–338.

Gardener, E. A. (2015). Abstinence-only sex education: College students' evaluations and responses. *American Journal of Sexuality Education, 10*(2), 125–139.

Garland-Thomson, R. (2002). Integrating disability, transforming feminist theory. *NWSA Journal, 14*(3), 1–32.

Gibson, B. E. (2006). Disability, connectivity and transgressing the autonomous body. *Journal of Medical Humanities, 27,* 187–196.

Gibson, B. E., Carnevale, F. A., & King, G. (2012). 'This is my way': Reimagining disability, in/dependence and interconnectedness of persons and assistive technologies. *Disability and Rehabilitation, 34*(22), 1894–1899.

Guldin, A. (2000). Self-claiming sexuality: Mobility impaired people and American culture. *Sexuality and Disability, 18*(4), 233–238.

Hansen, E. (2006). *Successful qualitative health research.* Buckingham: Open University Press.

Haraway, D. (1991). *Simians, cyborgs and women: The reinvention of nature.* New York, NY: Routledge.

Hirst, J. (2012). It's got to be about enjoying yourself: Young people, sexual pleasure, and sex and relationships education. *Sex Education: Sexuality, Society and Learning, 13*(4), 423–436.

Holt, L. (2010). Young people's embodied social capital and performing disability. *Children's Geographies, 8*(1), 25–37.

Hutchison, P. (2013). *Inquiry into improving child health outcomes and preventing child abuse, with a focus on pre-conception until three years of age.* Retrieved from http://www.parliament.nz/resource/0002018580

Kafer, A. (2003). Compulsory bodies: Reflections on heterosexuality and ablebodiedness. *Journal of Women's History, 15*(3), 77–89.

Kearney, A. (2009). *Barriers to school inclusion: An investigation into the exclusion of disabled students from and within New Zealand schools* (Unpublished PhD thesis). Massey University, Palmerston North.

Kewman, D., Warschausky, S., Engel, L., & Warzak, W. (1997). Sexual function in people with disabilities and chronic illness. In M. L. Sipski & C. J. Alexander (Eds.), *Sexual function in people with disabilities and chronic illness* (pp. 356–371). New York, NY: Aspen Publishers.

Kulick, D., & Rydström, J. (2015). *Loneliness and its opposite: Sex, disability, and the ethics of engagement.* Durham, NC: Duke University Press.

Lesko, N. (2010). Feeling abstinent? Feeling comprehensive? Touching the affects of sexuality curricula. *Sex Education: Sexuality, Society and Learning, 10*(3), 281–297.

McLaughlin, J., & Coleman-Fountain, E. (2014). The unfinished body: The medical and social reshaping of disabled young bodies. *Social Science & Medicine, 120*, 76–84.

Mcpherson, L. (2013). *The New Zealand disability survey 2013.* Wellington: Ministry of Health.

Mcruer, R. (2006). Compulsory able-bodiedness and queer/disabled existence. *The Disability Studies Reader, 4*, 88–99.

Moore, A. (2013). For adults only? Young people and (non)participation in sexual decision making. *Global Studies of Childhood, 3*(2), 163–172.

Oliver, M. (1990). *The politics of disablement (Critical texts in social work and the welfare state).* Basingstoke: Palgrave Macmillan.

Richardson, D. (2000). Constructing sexual citizenship: Theorizing sexual rights. *Critical Social Policy, 20*, 105–135.

Robinson, K. H. (2012). 'Difficult citizenship': The precarious relationships between childhood, sexuality and access to knowledge. *Sexualities, 15*(3–4), 257–276.

Samuels, E. (2013). Sexy crips, or, achieving full penetration. *Disability Studies Quarterly, 33*(3). Retrieved February 24, 2015, from http://dsq-sds.org/issue/view/104

Sanders, T. (2007). The politics of sexual citizenship: Commercial sex and disability. *Disability & Society, 14*(10), 439–455.

Shuttleworth, R. P. (2007). Disability and sexuality: From the medical model to sexual rights. In G. Herdt & C. Howe (Eds.), *21st Century sexualities: Issues in health, education and rights* (pp. 145–148). New York, NY: Routledge.

Stace, H. (2015). *Disability policy in New Zealand*. Retrieved from http://briefingpapers.co.nz/2015/02/disability-policy-in-new-zealand/

Swain, J., & French, S. (2000). Towards an affirmation model of disability. *Disability and Society, 15*(4), 569–583.

Sykes, H. (2009). The qbody project: From lesbians in physical education to queer bodies in/out of school. *Journal of Lesbian Studies, 13*(3), 238–254.

Tepper, M. S. (2000). Sexuality and disability: The missing discourse of pleasure. *Sexuality and Disability, 18*(4), 283–290.

The Education Act 1989. (1989). *Wellington: New Zealand government*. Retrieved from http://www.legislation.govt.nz/act/public/1989/0080/latest/DLM175959.html

Thomas, C. (2004). How is disability understood? An examination of sociological approaches. *Disability and Society, 19*(6), 569–583.

Van Amsterdam, N., Knoppers, A., & Jogmens, M. (2015). It's actually very normal that I'm different: How physically disabled youth discursively construct and position their body/self. *Sport, Education and Society, 20*(2), 152–170.

Wellings, K., & Field, B. (1996). Sexual behaviour in young people. *Bailliere's Clinical Obstetrics and Gynaecology, 10*(1), 139–160.

Wiegerink, D. J. H. G., Roebroeck, M. E., van der Slot, W. M., Stam, H. J., & Cohen-Kettenis, P. T. (2010). Importance of peers and dating in the development of romantic relationships and sexual activity of young adults with cerebral palsy. *Developmental Medicine and Child Neurology, 52*(6), 576–582.

Wiegerink, D., Roebroeck, M., Bender, J., Stam, H., & Cohen-Kettenis, P. (2011). Sexuality of young adults with cerebral palsy: Experienced limitations and needs. *Sexuality and Disability, 29*(2), 119–128.

Wight, D. (1999). The limits to empowerment based sexuality education. *Health Education, 99*(6), 233–243.

CHAPTER 9

Quality of 'Belonging' and Its Relationship to Learning

Case Studies of Three New Entrant Children and a 12-Year Old with Down Syndrome

Christine Rietveld

Belonging as a valued member in a regular classroom is critical for all children (Bronfenbrenner, 1986), but particularly for those with impairments (and other differences) that may place them at increased risk of exclusion from their peers (Macartney & Morton, 2011; Rietveld, 2008, 2010). Failure to belong as a valued member is likely to have negative implications for learning and development. Maslow (1970) argues that if children's fundamental needs are not fulfilled, such as food and shelter, acceptance and belonging, then they are less likely to be able to engage productively in higher-order learning because their energy is liable to be diverted into fulfilling those more fundamental needs.

Since a key function of schools is the facilitation of learning (Ministry of Education, 2016), a main focus of schooling needs to ensure that all children experience belonging. Children who do not belong as valued members where relationships are marked by warmth, reciprocity, trustworthiness and a level of stability within one or more peer cultures in the classroom are unlikely to fulfil their potential as learners (Nuthall, 2007; Rietveld, 2008). They may adopt less desirable roles (e.g. class clown) in order for them to feel successful and hence, included (Erickson, 1996). Such 'inappropriate' behaviour may result in teachers applying for extra teacher-aide hours for the individual child, to keep her/him more focussed on the learning process, but this may further deprive the child of the kind of belonging within the peer culture that he/she is seeking and which is supportive of learning.

In this chapter, I use case studies to highlight pedagogical practices that promote belonging in contrast to those that do not. Failure to belong as an integral, valued member of a peer group(s) and/or class also deprives children of experiences that support their learning. In addition, children who do not support their peers' belonging as valued members fail to learn the kinds of skills necessary for living in an increasingly diverse society (Carrington, MacArthur, Kearney, Kimber, Mercer, Morton, & Rutherford, 2012; Rietveld, 1999, 2010,

2014). For instance, in Rietveld's (1999) research, a group of new entrants included Jonathan, a boy with Down Syndrome (DS). They were playing the familiar game of SNAP. While each player accepted the implicit rule of putting down a card immediately following the previous player, Jonathan hesitated to put his card down, to which a peer responded to the group, "Just leave him out! He doesn't know how to play". Perhaps Jonathan's peers interpreted his hesitation as a disability to participation in the group? Their unanimous response of excluding Jonathan from more active educational inclusion not only deprived Jonathan of learning the concepts and skills to enhance his participation, but also deprived them of learning appropriate ways of interacting with Jonathan. Learning how to relate to a diverse range of people is part of the NZ Curriculum and is considered an essential competency for living in today's diverse society (Ministry of Education, 2016).

In addition, since the core of cognitive activity arises out of social participation with more skilled and responsive others within the child's zone of proximal development (Vygotsky, 1978), being excluded by peers at school passively or actively will interfere with optimal learning outcomes. A child who is excluded misses out on the potential support peers provide and/or opportunities, motivation, interest, information and encouragement conducive to participation and learning success (Kollar, Anderson, & Palincsar, 1994). Children learn to make sense of their world through joint activities with others, but if a child does not belong as a valued member and is not included in those processes (i.e. if the processes do not involve reciprocity), shared meanings as a precursor to enhanced learning do not occur. Furthermore, when the sharing of responsibility and ideas fail to occur for all children in the group, then learning is compromised for children with and without impairments (Rietveld, 2012) as was evident in the example of Jonathan. Children who do not experience belonging as valued equal members of the peer culture remain isolated, thus not only depriving each other of potentially enriching relationships, and acquiring new skills and knowledge but also defeating the aims of the Education Act (1989), the New Zealand Disability Strategy (2001) and New Zealand Curriculum Framework (1993), legislation and documents that support an inclusive society.

1   Case Studies: Children and Their School Contexts

For the purposes of this chapter, I focus on the kinds of 'belonging' that three 5-year old boys with DS experienced during their first week of school (Richard), first semester of school (Ian and Jonathan) and for 12-year old Rachel, her last term of primary school. The data for the boys were part of a larger study investigating their transition to school (Rietveld, 2002) and for Rachel, the interview data were part of a study concerning the short-term memory of children with and without DS (Grimley, 2012, unpublished). The children all attended regular primary schools of their parents' choice.

The boys with DS were observed through continuous narrative recording observations and semi-structured interviews were undertaken with all significant others (parents, teachers, aides, principals). Approximately 10 hours of observational data were collected for Richard and 100 hours each for Ian and Jonathan. Two half-hour interviews concerning Rachel's experiences of inclusion were undertaken with Rachel's mother. Rachel was present and added her voice to the discussion intermittently. The data were analysed inductively for themes and patterns, describing the kinds of 'belonging' and the underlying processes taking place. Comparisons were made between the children's experiences within the different school settings.

2   How Did the Children Experience 'Belonging?'

The pattern of interactions between each child with DS in each of the different school settings suggested different kinds of 'Belonging', which in all but one case study interfered with ongoing inclusion and learning.

2.1   *When Belonging is Limited*
i)   Belonging as a pet or an object/inferior member (Richard)
Richard was viewed as a much younger member whom his classmates dominated and manipulated (always kindly), but in a way that met their needs rather than Richards. For example;

> When Richard is reading and vocalising about the picture book he had selected, Louise starts turning the pages for him. Richard says "No" to her several times. Eventually Louise stops turning the pages but she shuts and removes his book and gives him another. Several older children enter, and two boys sit next to Richard. Richard gets excited about his book and calls out "snake!" as he shows the boys. They fail to notice and do not respond. One boy says to the other, "I'll look after Richard today". The second boy says, "No, just leave him".

Richard's real and potential contributions were ignored in favour of non-contingent helping interactions. It would appear that Richard's peers have assigned him the role of object. They took control of his behaviour, provided few opportunities for him to contribute and there was no reciprocity. This affected their getting to know him as an individual and establishing the common ground necessary for developing more mature forms of belonging.

This kind of belonging was encouraged by the Charity Discourse of Disability promoted by pertinent school staff. Children were expected to help Richard who was seen as a victim of circumstance (as they did) and procedures were set up to care for him. Older children were rostered at lunchtime to 'mind' Richard, which precluded his classmates forming friendships with him. Evidence that the children had internalised this model appeared when I asked a classmate if she ever played with Richard, and she replied, "We (our class of 5-year olds) can't (play with Richard) because other big children play with him all the time".

The overall outcome for Richard was increasing exclusion from his peer group. His parents moved Richard to another school about a year after Richard's entry. The parents were concerned that despite their best intentions, the school did not have the pedagogical and theoretical knowledge to support Richard's learning and inclusion. They perceived a disconnect between Richard's learning and that of his peers.

ii) *'Belonging' as deficit member/subordinate* (Jonathan)
This category involved peers assigning Jonathan the role of subordinate by taking on the role of 'mini' teacher or disciplinarian. Classmates aligned themselves with the role and status of the teacher as they attempted to impose the conventional school expectations on him. In the following incident, Rebecca 'disciplined' Jonathan to conform to the teacher's explicit rule (reading a book after the completion of story writing).

> Jonathan is reading the pile of class name-cards in the book corner. He looks at his own name card and says to himself, "That Jonathan". Rebecca who is next to him says, "Jonathan, read a book". Jonathan replies, "No". Rebecca says to him, "Read a book Jonathan. I'm trying to make you be good. Read a book now, Jonathan...read a book, Jonathan...read a book now, Jonathan. Jonathan says, "No!" Rebecca says, "Yes!" Jonathan continues reading the name cards.

In this excerpt, there is no reciprocity, shared meanings or validation of Jonathan's appropriate reading. It would appear that from Rebecca's perspective, Jonathan's behaviour is defective, something she confirms to him and attempts to rectify (his failure to read a book in the right place). She ignores Jonathan's appropriate behaviour (his reading in the correct location) and his engagement in the key purpose of the activity (reading). Like the teacher on previous occasions in this classroom, Rebecca has learnt that all children must conform to the explicit curriculum in the same way which means reading a book in the correct location as opposed to reading anything else. Her rigid application of this rule is interfering with Jonathan's social and academic learning and renders him an outsider. Engaging in the explicit curriculum in this way is set down by the teacher and reinforced by classmates who do not have an intellectual impairment. This dominant discourse makes it difficult for Jonathan to engage in the explicit curriculum and learn from it, as his deviancy is constantly emphasised thus interfering with any positive feedback, shared meanings and connectedness from his peers.

In this case, what contributes to Jonathan's experiences at the 'chalk face' is the school's discourse of disability that viewed 'inclusion as assimilation' into the existing school culture. The focus was on Jonathan's deficiencies as opposed to the school culture that did not cater for the range of children present. Children were publicly evaluated on a limited set of developmental criteria or required to engage in tasks in specific ways (e.g. read books rather than name cards) that were often unobtainable for Jonathan. This resulted in the exclusion of newcomers, particularly those with identifiable differences such as Jonathan who immediately appeared deficient. No attention to peer relationships or social norms meant that new children like Jonathan could not easily gain access to already-established friendship groups or the opportunities to belong as a valued member.

Once a child was viewed as 'deficient' or naughty by their peers, it became very difficult for that child to gain entry to a peer group. The following observation demonstrates that despite a child using competent social skills to gain entry, the discourse of deficit member precludes his inclusion.

> During a wet lunchtime, Jonathan sits on one of the seats around his set of 6 tables. Two girls are also seated here (these were the only seats left). A third girl sits opposite Jonathan. Jonathan says animatedly, "All by me!" (He seems excited about having the 3 girls sit by him). He takes out one of his marmite sandwiches and shows Millie next to him saying, "Look, I got marmite". She looks but doesn't respond verbally or emotionally [No validation of Jonathan's appropriate interaction]. The 3 girls talk together. Jonathan watches. He looks at Millie and says, "Juice" as he shows her his drink bottle. She looks at it, but there is no verbal or non-verbal interaction.
>
> Jonathan shows Millie his mouth full of marmite sandwich. She says, "Don't do that".

Jonathan asks, "Why?"
No response. She carries on eating.
Essentially the three girls talk amongst one another and Jonathan is excluded from the conversation.

Jonathan picks up a reading folder from one of the desks. He stands up and throws the reading folder in the air, laughing. A child takes the folder from Jonathan, returns it to the owner and he tells Jonathan to "Sit down and go eat your lunch".

The critical aspect to note is that after conventional attempts to become part of the group, Jonathan then takes on the role of clown. Given the peripheral role he is assigned, despite his appropriate strategies in the beginning of this scenario, it is hardly surprising that Jonathan attempts to engage in behaviours that he sees might increase his status. Initially, he comments to the group on how pleased he is to have the girls sit by him, but they do not reciprocate the sentiment. Then he uses a conventional strategy (shows his sandwich) to engage with Millie. However, his communication is ignored and the 3 girls talk amongst themselves. From then on, it would appear that Jonathan tries a number of unconventional strategies in an attempt to increase his membership of the group, all to no avail.

At the end of Jonathan's first semester of school, there was no visible academic progress and no development of relationships that involved mutual reciprocity and shared enjoyment. Jonathan's parents enrolled him at another school in an effort for him to experience the kind of inclusion they anticipated would be more supportive of his social and academic development.

iii)   When 'belonging' is not apparent (Rachel)
Rachel's experiences illustrate that in her peers' and teacher's minds, she is an extra who can be included if the situation allows it, but otherwise it is her parents' responsibility to ensure she is included and if they are unable, then she is not included. In the following incident, Rachel's classmates have arranged for the class to attend a local swimming pool for an end-of-year picnic and swim. As her classmates plan this activity, Rachel's (and possibly other children's) needs and abilities are not considered, nor do her teachers consider her inclusion as an issue that her peers need to consider in their planning. As Rachel's mother explained (when she was rung by the school about the end of year picnic), "The school contacted me and said that the end-of year class picnic at Sunsmart Pool wouldn't have a lot of supervision. When I suggested using teacher-aide hours [so that Rachel could participate], they said, We don't

have enough hours left'. " Rachel's mother took her daughter to the picnic and described Rachel's 'friends' as "busy" when they arrived, so Rachel asked to leave after she'd had a swim and had a look around. Rachel said, "I didn't like it". The school's response to Rachel's mother was "if she [Rachel] comes, she comes, if she doesn't, she doesn't. If you want her to go, you'll have to do it".

As can be seen in the example, Rachel's failure to belong as a valued member of the class after a whole year's participation in Year 8, is perpetuated at all levels of the school infrastructure and hence conveyed directly and indirectly to her classmates. Supporting Rachel's inclusion is not seen as a priority ("If she comes, she comes...if you want her to go, you'll have to do it"). This is hardly a warm welcome inviting Rachel's participation. She is clearly considered a low-status or inferior member of the class as opposed to a valued member. Supervision is not seen as the school's role, even though it is for her classmates, thus relegating Rachel to the role of an outsider as opposed to an integral member of the class. It would seem that her classmates have internalised that message – no consideration of all their classmate's abilities and viewpoints when considering options for their end-of-year venue. Rachel would appear to have internalised that view. Apart from exchanging a few pleasantries with her 'friends', she did not experience 'belonging' as an integral member as evidenced by her asking her mother to take her home.

Rachel's mother stated that the incident concerning the end-of-year picnic mirrored many school activities Rachel experienced or did not experience during her primary school years. Increasingly, Rachel spent more and more time in the school's 'Learning Centre' and less time included in the regular class as her teachers perceived that much of the school-work was "over her head". Rachel's opportunities for belonging as a valued member of the regular Year 8 class were therefore diminishing and she was seen more and more as a "guest".

3 When Belonging is Facilitated (and Experienced)

iv)   Belonging as a valued member (Ian)
From Ian's second week of school onwards, Ian started experiencing inclusion as an equal status participant. He engaged in the full range of roles typical for that setting including friendships and he made visible gains in reading, printing and giving news. By the end of his first term, Ian was also involved in play-dates with friends and classmates after school and he was the only child in this research study to do so. An illustration of the reciprocal nature of Ian and his peers' relationship that contributes to the group's maintenance of play follows.

Ian and his friends (Brendan, Philip and Alex) are playing soccer'. Ian is looking for the ball (in the wrong place) and says to himself, "Where's the ball gone?" Brendan finds it and gives it to Ian saying, "There Ian". Ian smiles at Brendan, then kicks it. Brendan gets it and kicks it back. Ian says, "Wow!" in response to Brendan's kick. Brendan, Philip, Alex and Ian all chase the ball, laughing as they do so. Philip has just about got the ball. Ian calls out to him enthusiastically, "Philip, get it! Get the ball!" All chase it.

In this incident, Ian engages in behaviours that are reinforcing to his peers. He praises their efforts, he acknowledges Brendan's contribution (giving him the ball when he was looking in the wrong place) and he joins the spirit of the game (laughs with group). His peers are also reinforcing by acknowledging his problem (searching for the ball), not putting down his efforts at finding the ball by searching in the wrong place (a potential site for exclusion), and kicking the ball to him. While they did not overtly praise his efforts during this excerpt, they regularly did so on other occasions. E.g. Philip to Ian, "Ian, Hey Ian. What a jolly good kick!"

Other aspects illustrating that Ian was experiencing facilitative inclusion included peers interpreting the likely intent of any unconventional behaviour and making the implicit, explicit, e.g. Ian vocalises/babbles to Philip while offering him a brown crayon while Philip is focused on his colouring in. Philip explains, "I don't need it. I don't need brown". Ian puts the crayon down.

As evidenced in the examples, Ian actually experienced 'Belonging' as a valued member and the wider school infra-structure facilitated these experiences through the immediate and distal school systems. Ian's teacher and teacher-aide changed the classroom culture by including additional criteria for children to reflect on when reporting back after choosing time activities. Not only did the teacher encourage the children to describe the block structure (or other activity), but to report on how well the participants worked together, who did what and how they resolved any difficulties. Children were therefore required to think about how they included their peers.

Throughout the day, everyday opportunities were used to help the children discover common ground facilitative of inclusion. Therefore, Ian's desk was placed amongst a group of peers who had interests in books, dinosaurs and balls. Activities also reflected these interests (e.g. the stories read) so that Ian would experience proximity of contact with potential friends and some of the children in his printing group were also selected to be in his reading and maths groups (to enhance familiarity and support authentic belonging).

Ian's teacher, aide, parents and principal supported a different set of beliefs about inclusion and disability based on an alternative model of disability (the social construction model; Shakespeare, 2014) which they consistently translated into practice at all levels of the school system. Their focus was on promoting a genuinely inclusive context from the outset to support the belonging and learning of all students. When potential difficulties were raised by Ian's parents such as how their son might experience inclusion at lunch time when they anticipated that he might have difficulty managing the static adventure playground, the school's response was to change the school culture in the junior area by incorporating activities that highlighted Ian's competencies and interests (soccer) in a way that made the overall class culture more inclusive for a greater number of children.

This particular case study provides an example of how children's authentic belonging within the peer culture can be facilitated. The processes Ian and his classmates experienced at the 'chalk face' were shaped at all levels of the schools' educational culture, which permeated through its practices and ethos of the school. These were based on the valuing of diversity as a prevailing norm, as opposed to deficiencies or problems. The children clearly internalised how to respond to Ian as an integral member of the class as this was the only school where classmates and friends regularly advocated for Ian when others engaged in unhelpful behaviour that negatively affected him. At one point, children were blocking access to the pigeon-holes where the lunch boxes were kept and Ian was stretching to reach his. Matthew called out to the group, "Hey, let Ian in".

4   Discussion

For children with identifiable differences to experience the kind of belonging that is conducive to their academic and social learning, they need to participate in classroom cultures that intentionally support such processes. A conscious decision to utilise a disability discourse that focuses on the quality of the child's educational context at all levels (e.g. parent-school meetings, decisions about how a teacher-aide is used), as opposed to her/his child's deficits is an essential starting point. Using a deficit discourse is likely to result in the kinds of exclusionary experiences illustrated in the first three case studies (Richard, Jonathan & Rachel), which focused on their assimilation into existing school cultures or being included as a pet/object. The pedagogical practices that focused on the individual as separate from his/her context contributed to these children remaining marginalised from any of the peer cultures operating in their classrooms and peers failing to develop an increasing range of appropriate skills to include their diverse classmates in mutually-satisfying and supportive ways.

5   Implications for Children

According to Vygotsky (1978), thinking develops through social experiences that are mediated through psychological tools consisting of language, concepts, symbols and skills. Children learn these tools through their participation and inclusion with more skilled members (adults and peers). Ongoing exclusion and/or low level inclusion is likely to result in the failure to learn culturally-valued tools because mental functions become altered as a result of the quality of the interaction (inclusion). The incident between Richard and classmate Louise illustrates this point. Louise turns over the pages of Richard's book and while he says, "No" she continues to do so. From this, Richard is likely to learn that he is incompetent and his agency at turning the pages when he sees it appropriate is not desirable. Using Vygotsky's model, ongoing experiences of this nature are likely to result in his mental functions becoming altered as a consequence of this type of inclusion. It is not the biological impairment itself that is hindering Richard's learning but the social implications of his peers and indirectly the distal contexts that impact on the quality of those peer interactions. Being in a relationship where one party such as Louise dominates on an ongoing basis provides insufficient mutually-satisfying shared connections for a relationship to develop and grow. From this encounter, Louise does not become aware of Richard's real interests and capabilities, but relates to him on a stereotypical level (poor little disabled/incompetent boy). Richard is perceived as an object that can be discarded as soon as other opportunities arise, as one child said to another when someone asked her to join her in an activity, "You can look after Richard now".

The experience of excluding the child with DS in its variety of forms leads the typically developing children to develop particular constructions about her/him. These primitive/limited constructions not only hinder the child with DS's social and academic experiences, but also their own learning and development. The typically developing children were learning by default that certain differences were negative and to be avoided. By positioning others as inferior, they were positioning themselves as superior. This kind of erroneous thinking hinders learning how to interact and feel comfortable with people with identifiable impairments or other differences, which in turn interferes with goals of social justice and learning how to live, work and learn in an increasingly diverse society (MOE, 2016). Learning how to include peers with impairments is a vital skill and outcome of educational inclusion that needs to be as much an integral component of children's socio-cultural contexts as learning to be bi-cultural as the modern workplace and community aspires to inclusive participation for all (diversityworksnz.org.nz). In three out of these four schools, the data indicated that this had yet to occur. Richard, Jonathan and Rachel were enrolled, but they did not experience the kind of belonging facilitative of their learning or growth in self-esteem.

6 Implications for Teachers and Schools

Leaving the quality of a child with DS's belonging/inclusion up to the child cannot be left to chance as can be seen by Richard, Jonathan and Rachel's experiences as they were included as marginalised, inferior members which interfered with other more enabling learning experiences. School contexts need to address the quality of all children's inclusion from the outset by focussing on all aspects of the schools' infrastructure.

The data indicate the need for teachers to expand their roles as part of teaching the explicit curriculum. For instance, teachers may need to consider how to include the child with DS who has little expressive speech at 'news time' and what this might mean for existing practices such as children presenting their news in pairs. Helping children 'belong' as valued members of one or more peer groups as a co-requisite to learning needs to be considered. In addition, altering pedagogical practices to enable more inclusive participation for all members would also be desirable. For instance, Ian's teacher added reporting on the quality of inclusion as an integral goal when children were required to report back to the class on their joint activities during developmental time (e.g. building of a block structure).

Including children with DS (and other differences) involves peers getting to know multiple aspects of the child's personality (Rietveld, 2002) and seeing beyond initial impressions to other attributes. Not only does this require helping the child discover commonalities, but encouraging talk about any concerns they may have. If these emerging constructions are not addressed, they tend to flourish through the peer group Rietveld (2010), resulting in the child's exclusion and peers failing to develop more mature understandings of the child and how they might include her/him.

For successful outcomes teachers need to address aspects of the 'hidden curriculum' (see Rietveld, 2010) such as social norms as the various peer cultures may not always be inclusive. If children are to experience facilitative inclusion, their teachers must be able to distinguish inferior from enhancing forms of inclusion and know what authentic belonging looks like from the outset in order to promote it.

In summary, it is helpful for all children to develop emotional connections with a peer or group(s) for optimal social and academic learning to occur. The implications are great for children with impairments who do not experience this kind of belonging because a failure to develop positive connections is likely to hinder their access to and learning of the explicit curriculum. Teachers therefore need to pay attention to the quality of relationships children develop. Ian's case study indicates that this is possible with positive outcomes not only for Ian, but for his classmates, teacher, the wider school environment as well as his family. However, pedagogical practices at all levels need to be underpinned by a discourse of disability that focuses on the social context as opposed to the 'deficit' individual who is expected to assimilate into existing cultural norms without a consideration of the appropriateness of those norms.

References

Bronfenbrenner, U. (1986). Alienation and the four worlds of childhood. *Phi Delta Kappan, 67*(6), 430–437.

Carrington, S., MacArthur, J., Kearney, A., Kimber, M., Mercer, L., Morton, M., & Rutherford, G. (2012). Towards an inclusive education for all. In S. Carrington & J. MacArthur (Eds.), *Teaching in inclusive school communities* (pp. 3–38). Australia: John Wiley & Sons Australia Ltd.

Education Act. (1989). *Sections 8, 9, 10: Statutes of New Zealand.*

Erickson, F. (1996). Inclusion into what? Thoughts on the construction of learning, identity, and affiliation in the general education classroom. In D. L. Speece & B. K. Keogh (Eds.), *Research on classroom ecologies: Implications for inclusion of children with learning disabilities* (pp. 91–105). Mahwah, NJ: Lawrence Erlbaum Associates.

Grimley, M. (2012). *Investigating the effectiveness of adaptive working memory training in a range of children with developmental disorders: A pilot study* (Unpublished raw data). University of Canterbury, Christchurch.

Kollar, G. M., Anderson, C. W., & Palincsar, A. S. (1994, March). *Power status and personal identity in small group problem-solving: The effects of social power and tasks specific agendas.* Paper presented at the Annual Conference for the National Association for Research in Science Teaching, Anaheim, CA.

Macartney, B., & Morton, M. (2011). Kinds of participation: Teacher and special education perceptions and practices of 'inclusion' in early childhood and primary school settings. *International Journal of Inclusive Education, 15*, 1–17.

Maslow, A. (1970). *Motivation and personality.* New York, NY: Harper & Row.

Minister for Disability Issues. (2001). *Making a world of difference: The New Zealand disability strategy.* Wellington: Ministry of Health.

Ministry of Education. (1993). *The New Zealand curriculum framework.* Wellington: Learning Media.

Ministry of Education. (2016). Retrieved from http://www.education.govt.nz/ministry-of-education

Nuthall, G. A. (2007). *The hidden lives of learners.* Wellington: NZCER Press.

Rietveld, C. M. (1999). "Just leave him out!" inclusion in the junior school classroom. What is involved? *Set, 1*, 1–8.

Rietveld, C. M. (2002). *The transition from preschool to school for children with down syndrome: A challenge to regular education?* (PhD thesis). University of Canterbury, Christchurch.

Rietveld, C. M. (2008). Contextual factors affecting inclusion during children's transitions from preschool to school. *Australian Journal of Early Childhood, 33*(3), 1–9.

Rietveld, C. M. (2010). Early childhood inclusion: The hidden curriculum of peer relationships. *New Zealand Journal of Educational Studies, 45*(1), 17–32.

Rietveld, C. M. (2012). 'Facilitative inclusion' in early childhood and new entrant classrooms. In B. Kaur (Ed.), *Understanding teaching and learning: Classroom research revisited* (pp. 201–212). Rotterdam, the Netherlands: Sense Publishers.

Shakespeare, T. (2014). *Disability rights and wrongs revisited* (2nd ed.). London: Routledge.

Vygotsky, L. S. (1978). *Mind in society: The development of higher mental processes.* Cambridge, MA: Harvard University Press.

Index

2E   75–78, 80, 82, 85

Ability   7, 15, 27, 31, 59, 60, 69, 81, 87–89, 97, 99, 100, 107, 109, 112–114, 117
Acceptance   27, 67, 108, 122
Achievements   35, 77, 81, 114
Active participation   56, 57, 60, 61, 64–66, 68
Adulthood   26, 107, 108
Adults   4, 25, 28, 30–32, 62, 63, 131
Aggressive   26
Anthropocene   17
Asexuality   107
Aspirations   56, 107, 115
Assessment   2, 30
Assistance   36, 49, 109
Assumptions   3, 6, 27, 29, 40, 42, 43, 45, 48, 52, 63, 65, 76, 83, 86, 88, 110, 118
Attendance   57, 58, 61, 65
Attitudes   57, 67, 116
Autism spectrum disorder   3, 25, 57, 82
Awareness   26, 79, 85, 86

Barriers   2, 5, 6, 8, 56, 57, 59, 63–67
Beliefs   5, 6, 18, 65, 83, 107, 130
Belonging   1–4, 17, 18, 25–29, 31, 32, 34, 37, 40, 42, 43, 49, 51, 52, 58, 60, 63, 95, 101, 102, 122–125, 127–130, 132, 133
Biases   42
Boundaries   30, 33, 34, 43
Bullying   33

Capabilities   75, 77, 78, 81, 89, 131
Challenges   1, 30, 37, 43, 49, 52, 67, 76, 82, 86, 98, 112
Child-care   13
Citizens   6, 14, 60–63, 87, 116
Citizenship   14, 56, 61–63, 65, 67, 68, 95, 108, 110
Classroom   15, 25, 27, 29, 31, 32, 37, 109, 110, 114, 115, 118, 122, 126, 129, 130
Climate change   2, 5, 16, 17
Cohesion   9, 15
Collaborative   49, 59, 68
Commodity   14
Community   2, 18, 25, 27–31, 34, 36, 37, 49, 52, 57, 58, 62, 63, 65–69, 101, 132

Community of Practice   62, 63, 66–69
Competent   58, 60–62, 65, 126
Competitiveness   75, 76, 91
Complexities   1, 25, 45, 98
Condition   25–27, 30, 116
Connections   2, 15, 97, 107, 110, 114, 115, 131, 133
Connectivities   109
Connotations   82, 112
Constrains   41
Constraints   2, 9, 42, 52
Construct   1, 3, 15, 42, 75, 77, 78, 88, 91, 101, 115
Construction   36, 43, 49, 75–78, 85, 88–91, 97, 102, 109, 111–114, 130
Constructionism   76, 77
Constructs   64, 68, 76, 78, 97
Contradictions   113
Curricula   59, 63
Curriculum   2, 14, 30, 34, 60, 61, 77–79, 87, 100, 111, 123, 126, 132, 133

Deaf   101
Deaths   7, 13
Decision making   6, 61, 62, 64, 65, 90
Deconstruct   46, 51, 100
Deconstruction   48
Defective   125
Deficient   88, 126
Deficit discourses   62, 65
Degradation   17
Democracy   1, 6, 17
Desirability   108
Developed world   12
Development   7, 8, 10, 15, 32, 35, 41, 42, 49–51, 59, 60, 65, 75, 79–81, 83, 99, 107, 122, 123, 127, 131
Developmentally curious   56
Differences   78, 87, 89, 90, 101, 122, 126, 130–132
Difficulty   27, 30, 31, 44, 60, 82, 130
Disability   4–7, 27, 30, 32, 57–62, 65–68, 82, 83, 85, 86, 95–99, 101, 107–118, 123, 125, 126, 130, 133
Disabled   4, 6, 15, 56, 58–61, 64–69, 85, 107–118, 131
Disadvantages   82
Discourses   1, 44, 45, 57, 61–63, 65, 95, 96, 101, 102

INDEX

Discriminated 15, 67
Discrimination 5, 10, 57, 59, 101
Disempowered 56
Disengagement 114
Disparities 14
Diverse 2, 25, 41, 50, 57, 63, 64, 79, 81, 83, 110, 113, 118, 122, 123, 131, 132
Diversity 2, 49, 57, 59, 60, 63–65, 67, 68, 76, 82, 83, 130
Down Syndrome 4, 122, 123

Early childhood education 2, 56, 59–61, 63–65, 67, 80
Ecological participation 61, 64
Education Act 30, 111, 123
Educator 46, 58, 62
Employment 11, 27, 49, 51, 78
Engage 11, 26, 31–34, 57, 61, 64, 114, 122, 126, 127
Engagement 1, 37, 60, 117, 118, 126
Engaging 31, 35, 56, 69, 81, 126
Enrolment 41, 61, 65
Equitable 2, 6, 59–66, 75, 101
Equity 1, 76, 91, 95, 101, 102
Ethnicity 5, 95–97, 100, 111
Exclusion 2, 5, 18, 49, 60, 101, 122, 125, 126, 129, 131, 132
Expectations 8, 41, 42, 108, 114, 116–118, 125
Exploitation 6, 118
Failure 1, 13, 16, 32, 33, 86, 101, 122, 125, 128, 131, 133
Fairness 1, 2, 18, 68
Freedom 8, 11, 16, 62, 66, 91
Friendships 29, 32, 35, 114, 115, 125, 128
Frustration 33, 86
Fundamentalism 10

Gap 37, 50
Gender 5, 48, 95–100
Gifted 75–87, 89–91
Giftedness 3, 75–80, 82–91
Global warming 14, 16, 17
Globalisation 11
Government 7, 9, 10, 12–14, 16, 41, 44, 63, 69, 77, 80, 81, 85, 87, 91

Health and Disability Act 7
Higher education 41, 81
Hopelessness 101
Huakina Mai 61, 65

Human rights 1, 7, 8, 56, 59, 63, 68
Humanising 67
Humanism 43, 48
Humanity 1, 2, 5, 17, 69

Identification 78, 81–84, 86, 87, 89, 99, 112
Identities 37, 40, 42, 95–101, 107, 111–113, 117, 118
Identity 1–4, 26, 40, 42, 43, 48–50, 62, 68, 96, 97, 100, 101, 107, 108, 111–118
Ideology 2, 6, 10, 16–18, 100
Impaired 114, 117, 118
Impairment 33, 60, 114, 116, 118, 126, 131
Implications 1, 30, 44, 46, 47, 75, 76, 89, 98, 109, 122, 131–133
Inappropriate 36, 122
Inclusion 1–12, 15, 18, 25, 28, 29, 37, 40–43, 48–51, 56, 60, 62, 67, 68, 75, 80, 95, 96, 101, 102, 110, 112, 123–133
Inclusive 1, 2, 4–8, 10, 13–15, 17, 18, 25, 27–30, 37, 40, 42, 48, 49, 51, 56, 58–69, 75, 78, 81, 89, 91, 95, 101, 102, 107, 110, 113, 118, 123, 130, 132, 133
Inclusive/equitable participation 64
Inclusiveness 3, 91
Incompetence 97
Independence 30, 108–110, 113, 114
Indifference 15
Indigeneity 82
Individualism 5, 10, 12, 17, 18
Inequality 6, 8, 10, 12–14, 17, 48, 96–100
Inferior 97, 101, 124, 128, 131–133
Inferiority 8
Inhibitions 109, 116, 117
Intelligence 85, 87, 88, 91
Interactions 1, 29, 31, 33, 36, 76, 84, 109, 117, 124, 131
Interpretations 42, 58, 64
Interpretivist 66
Intersectionality 3, 48, 95–102
Isolation 33

Judge 87
Justice 5, 8, 9, 14, 15, 17, 75, 77, 78, 85, 114, 131

Labelled 76, 77, 81, 84, 91, 98
Learning 1, 2, 4, 27–30, 32, 34–37, 40, 42, 46, 52, 56, 57, 59, 60, 62, 63, 65–69, 75–82, 84–88, 90, 91, 111, 112, 118, 122–126, 128, 130–133

INDEX

Learning needs   60, 79, 86, 90, 132
Life expectancy   9, 10, 12

Maori   6, 8–10, 69, 80, 82
Marginalised   1, 40, 51, 56, 91, 95, 97, 98, 100, 101, 130, 132
Measurement   78, 83, 84, 87–91
Medical model   85, 87, 88, 108
Medication   35
Meritocracy   77
Ministry of Education   60, 63, 65, 69, 75, 78–83, 85, 89–91, 122, 123
Minority   15, 90, 111
Modernity   114
Mortality   10, 13

Natural   63, 114
Neoliberal   2, 5, 10, 12, 13, 15–18
Neoliberalism   11, 12, 14, 17, 45
New Zealand Disability Strategy   5, 59, 123
Normalcy   43, 99, 101
Normality   101
Normativity   101

Objectivity   43
Opportunities   1, 2, 8, 34, 36, 37, 63, 68, 78, 81, 84, 91, 101, 123, 125, 126, 128, 129, 131
Opportunity   1, 29, 31, 35, 50, 59, 65, 75, 77, 110, 112, 113, 118
Oppression   3, 6, 11, 48, 64, 96, 97, 100
Oppressive   3, 90, 97, 101
Outcomes   11, 15, 30, 36, 37, 62, 77, 81, 85, 90, 96, 97, 99, 123, 132, 133

Paradigms   63
Parents   3, 14, 15, 26, 32, 35, 56, 62, 67, 68, 75, 76, 78, 79, 81, 82, 84–86, 88, 90, 91, 114, 115, 124, 125, 127, 130
Participation   2, 5, 8, 56–68, 75, 78, 91, 110, 114, 123, 128, 131, 132
Pedagogic participation   62, 63
Pedagogy   2, 66, 67, 75, 78, 109, 118
Peers   25, 28–30, 33, 34, 37, 44, 59, 65, 69, 87, 90, 107, 108, 111, 112, 115, 122–129, 131, 132
Personality   115, 132
PhD   3, 37, 40–42, 48–52, 76, 83
Pleasure   25, 29, 108–110
Policy   2, 3, 7, 9, 10, 13, 29, 60, 75–79, 83, 89, 91, 98, 99, 111, 113
Post modernism   43

Poverty   5–7, 11, 13–15, 17
Power   1, 5–8, 10–12, 17, 27, 29, 35, 43, 44, 46, 50, 63, 64, 66, 67, 97, 100
Powerless   82, 90
Preschool   56–58, 69, 84
Primary schools   32, 83, 84, 124
Priority   128
Private good   14, 15
Privatisation   12
Privileges   9, 36, 109, 113
Problem   40, 41, 45, 48, 69, 98, 100, 102, 129

Quality   4, 7, 29, 41, 59, 60, 64, 66–68, 80, 90, 114, 122, 130–133
Queen Street Project   40, 42, 49, 50–52
Queer studies   96

Race   9, 48, 95–100
Reciprocal   2, 68, 128
Recognition   9, 26, 78
Recommendations   13, 32, 90
Reconstructed   95, 102
Regional   81
Rejection   32, 114
Relationships   2, 10, 18, 26, 28, 32, 33, 35, 37, 59, 62, 66–99, 107, 110, 112, 115, 122, 123, 126, 127, 133
Representations   68, 115
Respectful   2, 62, 68
Responsive   2, 57, 68, 80, 123
Restrictions   8, 11
Rightness   5
Risk   1, 51, 122
Rural   81

Satisfaction   77, 118
Schooling   3, 40, 75, 78, 79, 88, 110–112, 122
Sex   115–117
Sexism   97
Sexuality   2, 4, 5, 96, 99, 100, 107–110, 115–118
Skills   27–30, 32–37, 42, 50, 62, 77, 78, 88, 89, 122, 123, 126, 131
Social capital   107, 110, 11
Social constructionist   75
Social good   10–15, 18
Social structures   48
Society   5–13, 15, 16, 59, 61, 63, 66, 77, 84, 88, 98, 108, 122, 123, 132
Special needs   60, 112
Specialised schools   25

Status   7, 95, 99, 125, 127, 128
Strengths   2, 29, 62, 86
Structuralism   43
Subjectivity   43, 46–48, 50, 62, 97, 109
Subordination   49, 101
Superior   100, 131
Support   1, 2, 7, 9, 10, 13, 15, 16, 27, 32, 37, 49, 57, 58, 60, 66–69, 79–84, 86, 87, 90, 91, 110, 112, 114–118, 122, 123, 125, 129, 130
Support worker   58
Supportive   40, 43, 49, 50, 65, 111, 122, 127, 131

Talented   79–83
Te Whariki   60
Teaching   7, 25, 32, 49, 56, 58, 60, 62, 65–68, 80, 82, 84, 89, 132
Tension   28
The Family Violence Death Review committee   7
The Ministry of Education's construction of giftedness   90
The Ministry of Education's Success for All policy   60
The United Nations Convention on the Rights of Persons with Disabilities   59

Thinking with theory   44–46, 49
Threatening   101
Transition   29, 81, 124
Treaty of Waitangi   6–9, 80
Trends   40, 43, 50, 51
Triggers   36
Twice exceptionality   3, 75, 77, 78, 81, 82, 84–86, 88, 89, 91

Uncertainty   62, 87
Under-achieving   81, 82
Unfit   88
United Nations   7, 8, 13, 29, 59, 65
University   9, 10, 12, 15, 40–42, 44, 48–51, 110
Unusual behaviour   25
Unwelcomed   101

Valued   1, 4, 13, 15, 41, 44, 57, 61, 63, 65, 68, 69, 77, 91, 110, 113, 122, 123, 126, 128, 129, 132
Values   5–7, 10, 14, 59, 63, 77, 79, 115

Welfare   11, 13, 14
Wellbeing/Well-being   1, 2, 6, 14, 17, 18, 32, 58, 77, 89